Integrated Noise Model (INM)
Version 6.0 Technical Manual

REPORT DOCUMENTATION PAGE

Form Approved
OMB No. 0704-0188

Public reporting burden for this collection of information is estimated to average 1 hour per response, including the time for reviewing instructions, searching existing data sources, gathering and maintaining the data needed, and completing and reviewing the collection of information. Send comments regarding this burden estimate or any other aspect of this collection of information, including suggestions for reducing this burden, to Washington Headquarters Services, Directorate for information Operations and Reports, 1215 Jefferson Davis Highway, Suite 1204, Arlington, VA 22202-4302, and to the Office of Management and Budget, Paperwork Reduction Project (0704-0188), Washington, DC 20503.

1. AGENCY USE ONLY (Leave blank)	2. REPORT DATE January 2002	3. REPORT TYPE AND DATES COVERED Final Dec 97 - Jan 02

4. TITLE AND SUBTITLE
Integrated Noise Model (INM) Version 6.0 Technical Manual

5. FUNDING NUMBERS
FA265/A2012

DTFA01-99-C-00003
Task Orders 1, 10, 13

6. AUTHOR(S)
Jeffrey R. Olmstead[2], Gregg G. Fleming[1], John M. Gulding[3] (FAA Program Manager), Christopher J. Roof[1], Paul J. Gerbi[4], Amanda S. Rapoza[1]

7. PERFORMING ORGANIZATION NAMES AND ADDRESSES
1 U.S. Department of Transportation
Research and Special Programs Administration
John A. Volpe National Transportation Systems Center
Acoustics Facility, DTS-34
Kendall Square
Cambridge, MA 02142-1093

2 ATAC Corporation
757 North Mary Avenue
Sunnyvale, CA 94085

8. PERFORMING ORGANIZATION REPORT NUMBER

9. SPONSORING/MONITORING AGENCY NAMES AND ADDRESS
3 U.S. Department of Transportation
Federal Aviation Administration
Office of Environment and Energy
800 Independence Avenue, S.W.
Washington, DC 20591

10. SPONSORING/MONITORING AGENCY REPORT NUMBER
FAA-AEE-02-01

11. SUPPLEMENTARY NOTES
4 CSC Corporation
Kendall Square
Cambridge, MA 02142

12a. DISTRIBUTION/AVAILABILITY STATEMENT This report is part of the INM 6.0 software release.	12b. DISTRIBUTION CODE

13. ABSTRACT (Maximum 200 words)

The Federal Aviation Administration, Office of Environment and Energy (FAA, AEE-100) has developed Version 6.0 of the Integrated Noise Model (INM) with support from the John A. Volpe National Transportation Systems Center, Acoustics Facility (Volpe Center) for development of the acoustic computation module, and from the ATAC Corporation for systems integration, development of the graphical interface, and methods for computing aircraft flight profiles and constructing flight paths, which are processed by the acoustics module.

This Technical Manual describes the core technical components in INM 6.0, including the flight-path methodology (Chapter 2), along with the basic methodology employed by the INM to compute noise levels or time-above metrics at a single, user-specified observer, or at an evenly-spaced, regular grid of observers (Chapter 3).

The noise/time computation methodology includes a description of: (1) computation of the flight-segment geometric and physical parameters; (2) flight-segment noise-level interpolation process; (3) atmospheric absorption adjustment; (4) acoustic impedance adjustment; (5) flight-segment noise-fraction adjustment for exposure-based metrics; (6) aircraft speed adjustment for exposure-based metrics; (7) lateral attenuation adjustment; (8) ground-based directivity adjustment for observers behind start-of-takeoff-roll, as well as for computing metrics associated with run-up operations; (9) metric computation process; and (10) development of a recursively-subdivided irregular grid methodology, which is used for computing noise contours (Chapter 4).

14. SUBJECT TERMS
Airport Noise, Computer Model, Noise Contours, Integrated Noise Model, INM, Noise-Level Prediction, Noise-Level Metric, Day-Night Average Sound Level, L_{dn}, Heliport Noise Model, FAR Part 150, Impact

15. NUMBER OF PAGES
110

16. PRICE CODE

17. SECURITY CLASSIFICATION OF REPORT Unclassified	18. SECURITY CLASSIFICATION OF THIS PAGE Unclassified	19. SECURITY CLASSIFICATION OF ABSTRACT Unclassified	20. LIMITATION OF ABSTRACT

PREFACE

The ATAC Corporation, the John A. Volpe National Transportation Systems Center Acoustics Facility (Volpe Center), and the Federal Aviation Administration (FAA) Office of Environment and Energy Noise Division (FAA AEE-100) have jointly prepared this document. It is published to serve as the Technical Manual for the FAA's Integrated Noise Model (INM) Version 6.0 computer software, which is used to predict noise impact in the vicinity of airports. The contents are current as of INM 6.0c. The INM 6.0 Technical Manual presents the methodology employed by INM to build aircraft flight paths and to compute noise-level and time-above metrics based upon the finite flight-segment data.

DISCLAIMER

This document was produced by ATAC Corporation staff, who are responsible for the facts and accuracy of the material presented herein. The contents do not necessarily reflect the official views or policy of the U.S. Department of Transportation or the Federal Aviation Administration. This INM Technical Manual does not constitute a standard, specification, or regulation.

TABLE OF CONTENTS

LIST OF FIGURES

LIST OF TABLES

1   INTRODUCTION

Since 1978, the FAA's standard methodology for noise assessments has been the Integrated Noise Model (INM). INM is a computer program used by over 700 organizations in over 50 countries to assess changes in noise impact resulting from: (1) new or extended runways or runway configurations; (2) new traffic demand and fleet mix; (3) revised routings and airspace structures; (4) alternative flight profiles; and (5) modifications to other operational procedures.

The guidance and underlying database/noise calculation methodology for INM are given in three related documents. These include the Society of Automotive Engineers (SAE) Aerospace Information Report (AIR), SAE-1845, titled "Procedure for the Calculation of Airplane Noise in the Vicinity of Airports". This document shares similar material with European Civil Aviation Conference (ECAC) Doc 29 and International Civil Aviation Organization (ICAO) Circular 205.

With the release of INM 6.0 in September 1999,[1] the FAA's Office of Environment and Energy (AEE-100), with the support of the U.S. Department of Transportation, John A. Volpe National Transportation Systems Center (Volpe Center) Acoustics Facility, enhanced the core capabilities in the model through the inclusion of one-third octave-band spectral data for each aircraft. For INM 6.0, this spectral database has facilitated two enhancements: (1) the ability to account for actual atmospheric absorption based on ambient temperature and relative humidity data provided by a user, and (2) the ability to compute C-weighted noise metrics. In the long term, the inclusion of aircraft spectral characteristics within INM will improve the ability of the program to model more complete acoustic phenomenon that may be specified in updates to the guidance documents listed above.

The ATAC Corporation, serving as the FAA's systems integrator for INM, extended the Windows-based graphical user interface that was developed for INM 5.0 to support the functions in INM 6.0. ATAC also updated methods for computing aircraft flight profiles and constructing flight paths, which are processed by the acoustic module.

This INM Technical Manual describes in Chapter 1 the metric types available for computation, in Chapter 2 the flight-path segmentation methodology, and in Chapter 3 the methodology employed to compute metrics at an evenly spaced regular grid of observer positions. Chapter 4 describes the methodology used to develop the recursively-subdivided irregular grid required for computing noise contours. The Appendices discuss the derivation of INM algorithms and the development of spectral classes.

1.1   Grid-Point Computations

INM computes a noise-level metric or a time-above metric in the vicinity of an airport. The metric is presented as numeric values at a regular grid of observer points, or as contour levels.

For regular grid computations, observer locations are arranged in the form of a user-defined rectangular grid of points, with fixed distances between the points. A regular grid can be rotated with respect to the coordinate system.

For irregular grid computations, observer locations are arranged in the form of a recursively-subdivided grid of points, with varying distances between points. Irregular grids are utilized for contour computations. The density of grid points is a function of a user-specified level of subdivision (called the refinement level), accuracy (called the tolerance), and the lowest and highest expected contour levels desired (called cutoff levels). In general, the contour accuracy increases as grid density increases.

The basic noise computation process used for the development of a recursively-subdivided irregular grid is similar to the process used for the development of a regular grid. In generating the irregular grid, a regular grid is first generated such that the distance between grid points is approximately one nautical mile. User-specified refinement level, tolerance, and program generated knowledge about noise-significant flights, directs the process of subdividing the regular grid to improve contour accuracy.

1.2 Metric Families

The noise-level and time-above metrics computed by INM 6.0 are associated with three fundamental groups or metric families. [2,3,4,5,6]

The first family of metrics is related to the A-weighted sound level, denoted by the symbol L_A. A-weighted sound levels de-emphasize the low and high frequency portions of the spectrum. This weighting provides a good approximation of the response of the human ear, and correlates well with the average person's judgment of the relative loudness of a noise event.

The second family of metrics is related to the C-weighted sound level, denoted by the symbol L_C. C-weighted sound levels retain the low frequency portions of the spectrum. This weighting is intended to provide a means of simulating human perception of the loudness of sounds above 90 decibels.

The third group of metrics is related to the tone-corrected perceived noise level, denoted by the symbol L_{PNT}. Tone-corrected perceived noise levels are used to estimate perceived noise from broadband sound sources, such as aircraft, which contain pure tones or other major irregularities in their frequency spectra.

1.3 Metric Types

Within the three metric families, INM computes three types of metrics: (1) exposure-based metrics, (2) maximum noise-level metrics, and (3) time-above or percent time-above metrics. The noise metrics supported by INM 6.0 are shown in Table 1-1.

Table 1-1 INM 6.0 Noise Metrics

Noise Family	Metric Type	Noise Metric	Flight Multiplier			Averaging Time (hr)
			Day	Evening	Night	
A-Weighted	Exposure Based	SEL	1	1	1	--
		DNL	1	1	10	24
		CNEL	1	3	10	24
		LAEQ	1	1	1	24
		LAEQD	1	1	0	15
		LAEQN	0	0	1	9
		User-defined	A	B	C	T
	Maximum Level	LAMAX	1	1	1	--
		User-defined	A	B	C	--
	Time-Above Based	TALA	1	1	1	--
		User-defined	A	B	C	--
		%TALA	1	1	1	--
		User-defined	A	B	C	--
C-Weighted	Exposure Based	CEXP	1	1	1	--
		User-defined	A	B	C	T
	Maximum Level	LCMAX	1	1	1	--
		User-defined	A	B	C	--
	Time-Above Based	TALC	1	1	1	--
		User-defined	A	B	C	--
		%TALC	1	1	1	--
		User-defined	A	B	C	--
Tone-Corrected Perceived	Exposure Based	EPNL	1	1	1	--
		NEF	1	1	16.7	24
		WECPNL	1	3	10	24
		User-defined	A	B	C	T
	Maximum Level	PNLTM	1	1	1	--
		User-defined	A	B	C	--
	Time-Above Based	TAPNL	1	1	1	--
		User-defined	A	B	C	--
		%TAPNL	1	1	1	--
		User-defined	A	B	C	--

1.3.1 Exposure-Based Metrics

The exposure-based metrics represent the total sound exposure for a given time period, usually 24 hours, based upon average annual day conditions at an airport.

INM standard sound exposure metrics are:

L_{AE} A-weighted sound exposure level
L_{CE} C-weighted sound exposure level
L_{EPN} Effective tone-corrected perceived noise level.

These standard sound exposure metrics are used by INM to generate average noise metrics by applying associated time-averaging constants and day, evening, and night-time weighting factors.

INM standard average-level metrics in the A-weighted family are:

L_{dn}	Day-night average noise level
L_{den}	Community noise equivalent noise level
L_{Aeq24h}	24-hour average noise level
L_d	15-hour (0700-2200) day-average noise level
L_n	9-hour (2200-0700) night-average noise level.

INM standard average-level metrics for the tone-corrected perceived family are:

L_{NEF}	Noise exposure forecast
L_{WECPN}	Weighted equivalent continuous perceived noise level.

The day, evening, and nighttime weighting factors and the time-averaging periods for these metrics are shown in Table 1-1.

In addition to INM standard sound exposure and average sound level metrics, user-defined metrics for the three families are available. A user specifies the time-averaging constant and the day, evening, and nighttime weighting factors. Although there are no standard average-level metrics in the C-weighted family because such metrics are not commonplace, the user has the ability to define user-specific C-weighted metrics.

1.3.2 Maximum Noise Level Metrics

The maximum noise level metrics represent the maximum noise level at an observer location, taking into account aircraft operations for a particular time period (e.g., 24 hours).

INM standard maximum noise level metrics are:

L_{ASmx}	Maximum A-weighted sound level with slow-scale exponential weighting characteristics,
L_{CSmx}	Maximum C-weighted sound level with slow-scale exponential weighting characteristics,
L_{PNTSmx}	Maximum tone-corrected perceived noise level with slow-scale exponential weighting characteristics.

In addition to INM standard maximum noise level metrics, user-defined metrics are available. A user specifies the time period for determining the maximum level.

1.3.3 Time-Above Metrics

The time-above metrics measure the time or percentage of time that the noise level is above a specified noise-level threshold, taking into account aircraft operations for a particular time period (e.g., 24 hours).

INM standard time-above metrics are:

TA_{LA}	Time that the A-weighted noise level is above a user-specified sound level during the time period,
TA_{LC}	Time that the C-weighted noise level is above a user-specified sound level during the time period,
TA_{PNL}	Time that the tone-corrected perceived noise level is above a user-specified noise level during the time period,
$\%TA_{LA}$	Percent of time that the A-weighted noise level is above a user-specified sound level during the time period,
$\%TA_{LC}$	Percent of time that the C-weighted noise level is above a user-specified sound level during the time period,
$\%TA_{PNL}$	Percent of time that the tone-corrected perceived noise level is above a user-specified noise level during the time period.

In addition to INM standard time-above metrics, user-defined metrics are available. A user specifies the time period for determining the time-above value.

Table 1-2 summarizes the metrics available in INM 6.0, including the corresponding ANSI metric names.

Table 1-2 Summary of INM Noise Metric Abbreviations and Definitions

Metric Type	INM Name	ANSI Name	Definition/Full Name
A-Weighted Noise Metrics			
Exposure Based	SEL	L_{AE}	A-Weighted Sound Exposure Level
	DNL	L_{dn}	Day Night Average Sound Level
	CNEL	L_{den}	Community Noise Equivalent Level
	LAEQ	L_{AeqT}	Equivalent Sound Level
Maximum Level	LAMAX	L_{ASmx}	A-Weighted Maximum Sound Level
Time-Above Based	TALA %TALA	TA_{LA} $\%TA_{LA}$	Time-Above / Percent Time-Above
C-Weighted Noise Metrics			
Exposure Based	CEXP	L_{CE}	C-Weighted Sound Exposure Level
Maximum Level	LCMAX	L_{CSmx}	C-Weighted Maximum Sound Level
Time-Above Based	TALC %TALC	TA_{LC} $\%TA_{LC}$	Time-Above / Percent Time-Above
Tone-Corrected Perceived Noise Metrics			
Exposure Based	EPNL	L_{EPN}	Effective Perceived Noise Level
	NEF	L_{NEL}	Noise Exposure Forecast
	WECPNL	L_{WECPN}	Weighted Equivalent Continuous Perceived Noise Level
Maximum Level	PNLTM	L_{PNTSmx}	Tone-Corrected Maximum Perceived Noise Level
Time-Above Based	TAPNL %TAPNL	TA_{PNL} $\%TA_{PNL}$	Time-Above / Percent Time-Above

1.4   Terminology

This section presents pertinent terminology used throughout the document. The terms are arranged alphabetically.

A-Weighted. A-weighted noise levels emphasize sound components in the frequency range where most speech information resides; yielding higher levels in the mid-frequency (2000 to 6000 Hz) range and lower levels in both low frequency and high frequency ranges. A-weighted noise level is used extensively in the U. S. for measuring community and transportation noise.

Acoustically Hard Surface. Any highly reflective surface where the phase of the incident sound is essentially preserved upon reflection; example surfaces include water, asphalt, and concrete.

Acoustic Impedance Adjustment. An acoustic impedance adjustment, computed as a function of observer temperature, pressure, and elevation, is applied to NPD noise levels. Acoustic impedance is the product of the density of air and the speed of sound.

Acoustically Soft Surface. Any highly absorptive surface where the phase of the incident sound is changed substantially upon reflection; example surfaces include ground covered with dense vegetation or freshly-fallen snow.

Airport Pattern. A defined flight path (ground track and altitude above the airport) used by aircraft for touch-and-go operations.

Aircraft Speed Adjustment. An adjustment made to exposure-based noise levels when aircraft speed differs from 160 knots, the reference speed for the INM NPDs.

Approach. A flight operation that begins in the terminal control area, descends, and lands on an airport runway, possibly exerts reverse thrust, and decelerates to taxi speed at some location on the runway.

Atmospheric Absorption. The change of acoustic energy into another form of energy (heat) when passing through the atmosphere. NPD data are corrected for atmospheric absorption in accordance with the Society of Automotive Engineers (SAE) Aerospace Recommended Practice (ARP) 866A[7] and SAE Aerospace Information Report (AIR) 1845[8].

Average Annual Day. The user-defined best representation of the typical long-term conditions for the case airport. These conditions include the number and type of operations, the routing structure, the temperature, and the atmospheric pressure.

C-Weighted. C-weighted noise levels, as compared with A-weighted noise levels, emphasize sound components between 100 Hz and 2 kHz. C-weighting is intended to simulate the sensitivity of the human ear to sound at levels above about 90 dB. C-weighted noise levels are commonly used for assessing scenarios dominated by low-frequency sound, e.g., locations behind start-of-takeoff roll.

Calibrated Airspeed (CAS). The indicated airspeed of an aircraft (as read from a standard airspeed indicator), corrected for position and instrument error. Calibrated airspeed is equal to true airspeed in standard atmosphere at sea level.

Case Analysis Window. The user-defined rectangular area around an airport within which a contour analysis is performed.

Circuit Flight. A flight operation that combines a departure from and an approach to the same runway, with level-flight and/or varying-altitude segments in between.

Contour. An analysis of an area in the vicinity of an airport encompassed by a graphical plot consisting of a smooth curve, statistically regressed through points of equal noise level or time duration. There are two kinds of contour analyses: single-metric and multi-metric.

Corrected Net Thrust Per Engine. The net thrust per engine divided by the ratio of the ambient air pressure at aircraft altitude to the International Standard Atmosphere (ISA) air pressure at mean sea level.

Cutoff Levels. A test that determines when to end noise level (or time) computations during a single-metric contour analysis. The point at which computations are stopped is based on user-defined lowest and highest noise level (or time) contours. Similar to the tolerance and refinement level tests, the reason for performing this test is to reduce runtime during a single-metric contour analysis.

Decibel (dB). A unit of measure for defining a noise level or a noise exposure level. The number of decibels is calculated as ten times the base-10 logarithm of the ratio of mean-square pressure or noise exposure. The reference root-mean-square pressure is 20 μPa, the threshold of human hearing.

Departure. A flight operation that begins on a runway, proceeds down the runway, and climbs and accelerates to altitudes at specified distances.

Directivity Adjustment. A noise level adjustment resulting from the normalized noise pattern defined by a 360-degree area in the horizontal plane around a noise source. In INM, measurement-based directivity is accounted for in takeoff ground roll and runup operations.

Distance Duration. An empirically-derived effect, expressed as a function of distance, which relates exposure-based noise levels to maximum-based noise levels. This effect is taken into account in the INM NPD data only for data corrected using the simplified data adjustment procedure.

Extended Flight-Path Segment. A mathematical extension from either end of a geometrical flight-path segment to infinity.

Flight Operation. There are five kinds of flight operations in INM: approach, departure, touch-and-go, circuit flight, and overflight.

Flight Path. A set of flight path segments describing geometrical and physical parameters used to model the movement of an aircraft in three-dimensional space.

Flight Path Segment. A directed straight line in three-dimensional space, which includes the aircraft speed and corrected net thrust per engine at the beginning point of the line, and change in speed and thrust along the line to the end point.

Flight Profile. A set of points that models the geometrical and physical characteristics of an aircraft flight operation in the vertical plane. Each profile point contains: (1) the ground distance (x-value) relative to the origin of the operation, (2) the aircraft altitude above field elevation, (3) the aircraft true airspeed, and (4) the corrected net thrust per engine or equivalent parameter used to access the NPD curves.

Ground Plane. Without terrain elevation processing, the ground plane is the geometrical horizontal plane at the elevation of the airport. With terrain elevation processing, the elevation of the ground plane is determined using three-by-three arc-second geodetic elevation data for the area surrounding the airport.

Ground Speed. That component of aircraft speed obtained by projecting the aircraft velocity vector on the horizontal plane.

Ground Track. The trace of the flight path on the horizontal plane. Flight tracks are described as vector-type tracks consisting of one or more straight or curved segments, or point-type tracks consisting of an array of x,y points.

Integrated Adjustment Procedure. The preferred adjustment procedure used for developing INM NPD data from measured noise level data. It is based on noise level data measured over the full spectral time history of an event. In the integrated procedure, off-reference aircraft speed, atmospheric absorption effects, and spherical divergence are considered. This adjustment procedure provides data consistent with Type 1 quality, as defined in SAE-AIR-1845.[8]

International Standard Atmosphere (ISA). Internationally standardized functions of air temperature, pressure, and density versus aircraft altitude above mean sea level. The ISA is intended for use in calculations in the design of aircraft, in presenting test results of aircraft and their components under identical conditions, and to facilitate standardization in the development and calibration of instruments.[9]

Lateral Attenuation Adjustment. An adjustment that results from the attenuation of noise at grid points laterally displaced from the ground projection of an aircraft flight path. It is a combination of the ground-to-ground attenuation and the air-to-ground attenuation.

Maximum Noise Level. The maximum of a series of measured sound pressure levels from a single flight.

Mean-Squared Sound Pressure. A running time-average of frequency-weighted, squared instantaneous acoustic pressure. For example, A-weighted (denoted by subscript A) mean-squared pressure using slow (denoted by subscript S) exponential time averaging ($t_o = 1$ second) is calculated by:

$$p(t)_{AS}^2 = \int_{-\infty}^{t} p_A^2(\tau)\, e^{\tau/t_o}\, d\tau / t_o$$

Mean-Square Sound Pressure Ratio. The mean-square sound-pressure ratio is the ratio of the mean-squared sound pressure divided by the square of the reference pressure 20 μPa. It is equivalent to $10^{SPL/10}$, where SPL is the sound pressure level.

Metric Family. A set of noise-level and time-above metrics differentiated by frequency weighting, either A-weighted, C-weighted, or tone-corrected perceived.

Metric Type. A metric belongs to one of three types: exposure-based, maximum-level, or time-above.

Multi-Metric. A contour analysis in which noise and time values are computed for three base metrics belonging to either the A-weighted or tone-corrected perceived family of metrics. The three primary metrics are the exposure-based, the maximum noise level, and the time-above metrics.

Noise. Any unwanted sound. "Noise" and "sound" are used interchangeably in this document.

Noise Fraction. The ratio of noise exposure at a grid point due to a flight segment, and the noise exposure at the same grid point due to a straight, infinite flight path extended in both directions from the segment. The noise fraction methodology is based upon a fourth-power 90-degree dipole model of sound radiation. It facilitates the modeling of a three-dimensional flight path, using straight flight segments.

Noise Fraction Adjustment. An adjustment that is a function of the ratio of the noise exposure at a grid point due to a flight-path segment, and the noise exposure at the same grid point due to a straight, infinite flight path, extended in both directions from the segment.

Noise-Level Threshold. A noise level specified by the user that is the boundary value above which time-above calculations are performed.

Noise-Power-Distance (NPD) Data. A set of noise levels, expressed as a function of: (1) engine power, usually the corrected net thrust per engine; and (2) distance. The INM NPD data are corrected for aircraft speed, atmospheric absorption, distance duration, and divergence.

Noise Significance Tests. Tests performed by INM to determine if a flight operation is acoustically significant. Two types of tests are used: the relative noise-level/time test and the segment proximity test. The reason for performing these tests is to decrease runtime during a contour analysis.

Observer. A receiver or grid point at which noise or time values are computed.

Overflight. A flight operation that begins in the air, and remains in the air, in the vicinity of the airport, with optional user-specified changes in altitude and speed during the flight.

Percent Time-Above. The percentage of time that a time-varying sound level is above a given sound level threshold.

Procedure Steps. A prescription for flying a profile. Procedures include climbing at constant calibrated airspeed to a given altitude, accelerating to a given airspeed while climbing at a given vertical rate, etc.

Profile Points. See Flight Profile.

Recursively-Subdivided Irregular Grid. A grid of observer points created by one or more subdivisions of an existing regular or irregular grid, based on the user-specified refinement level and tolerance.

Refinement Level. The number of levels of subdivision of a regular grid making up a recursively-subdivided irregular grid. Each successive refinement level beyond level three represents one level of subdivision.

Reference Day. The atmospheric conditions corresponding to 77 degrees Fahrenheit (25 degrees Celsius), 70 percent relative humidity, and 29.92 in-Hg (760 mm-Hg). These are the atmospheric conditions to which aircraft noise certification data are corrected in accordance with Federal Aviation Regulation Part 36.[10] These conditions are commonly referred to as ISA plus 10 degrees Celsius (ISA+10).

Reference Speed. The noise-exposure reference speed in INM is 160 knots. Thus, L_{AE} and L_{EPN} values in the NPD database are referenced to 160 knots. The L_{ASmx}, L_{CSmx}, and L_{PNTSmx} values are assumed to be independent of aircraft speed.

Regular Grid. A noise analysis of one or more noise-level and/or time-above metrics, for a set of observer points spaced at fixed intervals, over a specified area in the vicinity of the case airport.

Relative Noise-Level/Time Test. A noise significance test in which all flight segments of all operations are sorted high-to-low according to the noise (time) contribution of each segment at a regular grid point. Segments considered significant are those whose cumulative noise (time) first equals or exceeds 97 percent of the total mean-square sound-pressure ratio (total time) at the grid point.

Runup. An activity in which an aircraft is in a stationary position on the ground, with aircraft thrust held constant for a time period.

Segment Proximity Test. A noise significance test in which a flight segment, which is first determined to be insignificant by the flight segment noise test, is further tested based on its distance to a regular grid point. If it is determined that the flight segment is within a certain distance of the grid point, the flight segment regains its significance status.

Simplified Adjustment Procedure. An adjustment procedure used for developing INM data from measured noise level data. In contrast to the integrated procedure, the simplified procedure is based on noise-level data measured at the time of the maximum noise level only. In the simplified procedure, off-reference aircraft speed, atmospheric absorption, distance duration effects, and spherical divergence are considered. This adjustment procedure provides data consistent with Type 2 quality as defined in SAE-AIR-1845.[8]

Single-Metric. A contour analysis in which noise or time values are computed for a single, user-specified metric.

Sound Pressure Level (SPL). Ten times the base-10 logarithm of the ratio of the mean-squared sound pressure, in a stated frequency band, to the square of the reference sound pressure of 20 μPa, which is the threshold of human hearing.

$$SPL = 10 \log_{10}[p^2 / p_o{}^2]$$

where
p^2 mean-squared pressure (Pa^2),
p_o 20 μPa.

Sound Exposure (Noise Exposure). The integral over a given time interval ($t_2 - t_1$) of the instantaneous, frequency-weighted, squared sound pressure:

$$E_{12} = \int_{t_1}^{t_2} p^2(t)\, dt$$

Sound Exposure Level. Ten times the base-10 logarithm of the sound exposure divided by a reference sound exposure.

$$L_E = 10 \log_{10}[E/E_o]$$

where
E sound exposure (Pa^2s),
E_o (20 μPa)^2(1 s) for A-weighted and C-weighted sound exposure,
E_o (20 μPa)^2(10 s) for tone-corrected perceived sound exposure.

Sound Exposure Ratio. Commonly called "energy". The ratio of sound exposure over a reference sound exposure, or ten raised to power of one tenth the sound exposure level:

$$E/E_o = 10^{L_E/10}$$

where

E sound exposure (Pa^{2}s),

E_o reference sound exposure (Pa^{2}s),

L_E sound exposure level (dB).

Spectrum. A set of sound pressure levels in component frequency bands, usually one-third octave bands.

Spectral Class. A set of aircraft spectra which are grouped together based on similar spectral characteristics.

Spherical Divergence. Spherical divergence, which is taken into account in the INM NPD data, is defined as the transmission loss of mean-square sound pressure, which varies inversely with the square of the distance from a point source. In contrast, cylindrical divergence is the transmission loss of mean-square sound pressure, which varies inversely with distance from a line source.

Standard Day. The atmospheric conditions corresponding to 59 degrees Fahrenheit (15 degrees Celsius), 70 % relative humidity, and 29.92 in-Hg (760 mm-Hg). The values for temperature and atmospheric pressure are sea-level conditions for the International Standard Atmosphere (ISA).

Time-Above. The duration that a time-varying sound level is above a given sound level threshold.

Time-Averaging Constant. A constant decibel value that is ten times the base-10 logarithm of the time interval associated with the metric divided by a reference time interval, which is usually one second. For example, the time constant for L_{dn} is equal to 10 $\log_{10}$[86400 seconds in 24 hours / 1 second] = 49.37 dB. The time-averaging constant is subtracted from the sound exposure level to compute an equivalent or average sound level.

Tolerance. The allowable maximum difference in dB or minutes between computed noise or time values and linearly-interpolated noise levels or time values at a given observer point.

Tone-Corrected Perceived. Tone-corrected perceived noise levels are used to estimate human-perceived noise from broadband sound sources, such as aircraft, which contain pure tones or other major irregularities in their frequency spectra.

Touch-and-Go. A flight operation that begins with a level flight in the terminal control area, descends and lands on an airport runway, and then takes off immediately after landing and returns to level flight.

True Airspeed (TAS). The speed of an aircraft relative to the undisturbed air mass.

Weighting Factor. A numeric value that multiplies the sound exposure ratio associated with a time period for a given metric. For the exposure-based metrics, the weighting factor acts as a penalty for operations that occur during a specific time period. Usually larger penalties are applied during the night-time period when people are most sensitive to noise. For the maximum-level and time-above metrics, the weighting factors are either zero or unity. As such, they act as a binary switch allowing the user to select specific time periods for computation.

1.5 Abbreviations

This section presents various abbreviations and acronyms used in the document.

AFE	above field elevation (aircraft altitude)
AIR	Aerospace Information Report (SAE-AIR)
ARP	Aerospace Research Report (SAE-ARP)
C	degrees Celsius (temperature)
CAS	calibrated airspeed (corrected indicated airspeed)
CPA	closest point of approach to a line segment
dB	decibel (unit of sound level or sound exposure level)
F	degrees Fahrenheit (temperature)
F_n/δ	corrected net thrust per engine (pounds)
ft	feet
in-Hg	inches of mercury (barometric pressure)
INM	Integrated Noise Model
km	kilometers
kt	knots (international nautical miles per hour)
lb	pounds force or weight
L_{ASmx}	maximum A-weighted sound level, dB re $(20\ \mu Pa)^2$
L_{CSmx}	maximum C-weighted sound level, dB re $(20\ \mu Pa)^2$
L_{PNTSmx}	maximum tone-corrected perceived noise level, dB re $(20\ \mu Pa)^2$
L_{AE}	A-weighted sound exposure level, dB re $(20\ \mu Pa)^2(1\ s)$
L_{CE}	C-weighted sound exposure level, dB re $(20\ \mu Pa)^2(1\ s)$
L_{EPN}	effective tone-corrected perceived noise level, dB re $(20\ \mu Pa)^2(10\ s)$
m	meters
MSL	mean sea level (altitude above mean sea level)
nmi	international nautical miles (1852 m)
Pa	pascal (unit of pressure, one newton per square meter)
PCPA	perpendicular closest point of approach to an extended line segment
re	relative to
s, sec	second (time duration)
SAE	Society of Automotive Engineers
TAS	true airspeed

2   FLIGHT-PATH COMPUTATION METHODOLOGY

The fundamental components for computing noise in INM are a flight path segment and an observer. For a given observer location, noise computations are performed on a flight-segment by flight-segment basis. This Chapter presents the methods used to compute flight path segments, and Chapter 3 presents the methods used to compute noise at an observer position.

Chapter 2 has four sections:

Section 2.1 summarizes all the input data that are required for noise computation.

Section 2.2 discusses the input database used in conjunction with a flight path or runup position to compute noise at an observer position.

Section 2.3 presents methods used to calculate a flight profile, based on profile procedure steps.

Section 2.4 presents methods used to merge ground tracks with flight profiles to produce three-dimensional flight path segments.

2.1   Summary of Input Data for Noise Computation

The noise computation process requires case information about airport conditions, aircraft types, operational parameters, geometry between the observer/flight-segment pair, and noise metric information. Appendix A presents an example file of these data.

2.1.1 Airport Information

The following airport information is required for noise computations:
   Latitude and longitude of the airport reference point (decimal degrees);
   Runway end-point x,y positions relative to the reference point (feet);
   Airport elevation (feet MSL);
   Airport average annual day temperature (degrees Fahrenheit);
   Airport average annual day relative humidity (percent), when the atmospheric absorption
      correction is invoked;
   Airport average annual barometric pressure (inches of mercury re MSL).

As an option, terrain data can be used in the noise computations. Terrain elevation data are provided in one or more "3CD" files. Terrain elevations are given in meters 3 arc-seconds apart. A single 3CD file covers one degree in latitude by one degree in longitude (1201 x 1201 points). The spacing between points depends on the specific location. For example, the spacing in the Boston area is about 224 feet in the x (east-west) direction by 304 feet in the y (north-south) direction, while the spacing in the San Francisco area is about 241 feet by 303 feet.

The accuracy of U.S. terrain data is typically within 10 feet of actual elevation. However, inaccuracies of a large as 70 feet have been documented. Nevertheless, in areas of varying elevations, improvements in INM computational accuracy are obtained when the terrain enhancement is invoked.

2.1.2 Aircraft Information

The following aircraft information is required for noise computations:

Aircraft flight operation type: approach, departure, touch-and-go, circuit flight, overflight, or runup.

Number of flight operations for each of three time periods (day, evening, and night) during an average annual day.

For a flight operation, the three-dimensional flight path of the aircraft, as represented by a series of straight-line flight path segments containing position, direction, length, speed, and thrust information. Sections 2.3 and 2.4 present details of how a three-dimensional flight path is constructed.

For a runup operation, the position of the aircraft on the runup pad (x,y values in feet), the aircraft heading (degrees clockwise from true north), the corrected net thrust per engine (pounds or percent), and the duration of the runup operation (seconds).

NPD data, as presented below in Section 2.2.

2.1.3 Observer Information

Information about observer locations is required for noise computations. INM observer locations are expressed in the form a regular grid of points or a recursively-subdivided irregular grid of points.

Observer locations for a regular grid are defined by the location of the lower-left corner of the grid (feet), the distance between grid points in the two directions (feet), the number of grid points in the two directions, and the angle that the grid is rotated relative to the x-y axes (degrees counter-clockwise).

A special case of a regular grid is a grid consisting of a single observer location, in which the starting point for the grid is given, the distance between grid points is zero, and the size of the grid is one-by-one.

The computation of "population points" and "locations points" are also performed by using the single-grid-points method. The number of single points is an input parameter and their x,y values are listed in the input file.

Recursively-subdivided irregular grid points are generated by an algorithm that is based on a regular grid, as explained later in Chapter 4. The observer locations for the grid are determined by four corner points of the case analysis window and by a grid spacing of one nautical mile that is recursively subdivided into smaller grids.

2.1.4 Noise Metric Information

The following noise metric information is required for noise computations:

The type of computation: single-metric or multi-metric. A single-metric run can compute regular grid points and/or contours. A multi-metric run can compute only contours.

If a single-metric run is selected:
    metric identifier (DNL, SEL, etc.),
    metric type (exposure-based, max-level, time-above),
    metric weighting factors (day, evening, night),
    for an exposure-based metric, the averaging time constant (dB),
    for a time-above metric, the threshold level(s) (dB).

If a multi-metric run is selected:
    noise family type (A-weighted, C-weighted, or tone-corrected perceived),
    time-above noise-level threshold(s) (dB).

An indicator (yes or no) that contours are to be generated, using the recursively-subdivided grid method of calculating noise.

If contours are to be generated, the following parameters are required:
    refinement level,
    tolerance value (dB or minutes).

If contours are to be generated and if doing a single-metric run, the following parameters are required:
    low cutoff contour level (dB or minutes),
    high cutoff contour level (dB or minutes).

2.2   Input Database

INM contains an acoustic database of noise vs. power vs. distance (NPD) values, augmented by a database of spectral characteristics. The NPD data for an aircraft, which is usually obtained from the INM database but can be user-defined, consists of a set of decibel levels for various combinations of aircraft engine power states and distances from observer to aircraft. An underlying assumption is that the NPD data represent an aircraft proceeding along a straight flight path of infinite length and parallel to the ground.

The spectral data consist of a set of sound pressure level vs. one-third octave-band frequency (50 Hz to 10 kHz) values measured at the time of L_{ASmx} and corrected to a reference distance of 305 meters using the SAE AIR-1845 atmospheric absorption coefficients. These spectral data are used to compute actual atmospheric absorption based on airport temperature and relative humidity. The spectral data are also used to compute C-weighted noise metrics.

2.2.1 NPD Data Sets

Four kinds of NPD input data sets are available:

L_{AE} A-weighted sound exposure level,

L_{ASmx} Maximum A-weighted sound level with slow-scale exponential time weighting,

L_{EPN} Effective tone-corrected perceived noise level,

L_{PNTSmx} Maximum tone-corrected perceived noise level with slow-scale exponential time weighting.

All metrics in INM, including C-weighted and time-above metrics, are computed using these four basic noise-level metrics.

Normal NPD data consist of two or more noise curves. A noise curve is associated with an engine power parameter (in units of pounds or percent corrected net thrust of some other power state parameter), an operational attribute, either departure or approach, and noise levels at the following ten distances: 200, 400, 630, 1000, 2000, 4000, 6300, 10000, 16000, and 25000 feet.

To obtain noise levels that lie between thrust values or between distance values, linear interpolation on thrust and logarithmic interpolation on distance are used. Extrapolation is used to obtain levels outside of the bounding thrust or distances values, as discussed in Section 3.3.

Afterburner NPD data are also available for some NOISEMAP[11] aircraft.

The noise levels in the NPD data have been adjusted for time-varying aircraft speed (exposure-based noise levels only), atmospheric absorption, distance-duration effects (if the simplified adjustment process is used for exposure-based noise levels), and spherical divergence in accordance with the methodology presented in Reference 8 and summarized in Reference 12.

For NOISEMAP military aircraft, NPD data were developed using the simplified data adjustment procedure, and distance duration effects were computed using an empirically-derived $6.0 \log_{10}[d/d_{ref}]$ relationship. In contrast, NPD data for civilian aircraft that were corrected using the simplified procedure were adjusted using an empirically-derived $7.5 \log_{10}[d/d_{ref}]$ relationship. It was decided that the 6-log relationship would be maintained for the military aircraft in INM, since it represents a best-fit empirical relationship for those aircraft.

2.2.2 Spectral Data Sets

A spectral class is used to represent the spectrum at time of maximum sound level for a group of aircraft deemed to have similar spectral characteristics. The starting point in any empirical model such as INM is a reference database. In Version 5.2 and earlier, the reference noise database consisted of noise level data expressed as a function of aircraft power and aircraft-to-receiver distance, i.e., noise-power-distance (NPD) data. The addition of spectral class data in Version 6.0 allows INM to account for actual atmospheric absorption based on airport temperature and relative humidity data provided by a user. Spectral classes also give a user the ability to compute C-weighted noise metrics.

Reference 12, which is the source for most NPD curves developed prior to INM version 6.0, also contains one-third octave-band spectra (50 Hz to 10 kHz) measured at the time of L_{ASmx} and corrected to a distance of 305 m using the SAE AIR-1845 atmospheric absorption coefficients. For aircraft developed for INM 6.0 and later, the INM database request form (See Appendix E) has been updated to request the one-third octave band data necessary for determining a spectral class.

Similar spectral data for military aircraft were taken from the Noisefile Database in the United States Air Force NOISEMAP computer program. NOISEMAP is used for computing noise exposure at facilities dominated by military operations. The military data also exist in the form of one-third octave-band spectra measured at the time of L_{Asmx}. These data were corrected to a distance of 305 m using the SAE AIR-1845 atmospheric absorption coefficients to maintain similarity with Reference 12.

Although the above references included spectral data for the majority of INM aircraft, it is not considered necessary to support a separate spectrum for each INM aircraft. Based on validation tests, it was determined that maintaining separate spectral data for each aircraft would result in a negligible improvement in computational accuracy, whereas grouping similar spectra offers the desired enhancement for more advanced acoustical algorithms. Based on the above sources, Reference 13 provides the spectral class assignments for INM aircraft developed before Version 6.0. Aircraft added to INM since the release of Version 6.0 have been found to fit within spectral classes developed for Reference 13. Appendix D presents an overview of the development of a spectral class.

Sensitivity and validation tests were conducted to identify spectra that could be grouped together, referred to herein as a "spectral class". Aircraft were first grouped together by engine type and/or number of engines (i.e., low-bypass ratio jet, high-bypass ratio jet, four engine jet, turboprop, piston, etc.), and then the groups were broken down further by spectral shape. Some groups were partitioned further to eliminate the presence of widely used aircraft in the same group. For instance, the 737300 and the MD80 were placed in separate groups, even though their spectral shapes are similar.

Once the spectra were grouped together, a representative spectrum was determined for the group. The spectrum was calculated from a departure-weighted arithmetic average of the individual aircraft spectra in the group for commercial aircraft. For military aircraft, aircraft inventory data were collected and each spectral class was represented by the single military aircraft which had the highest number in inventory. Some single- and twin-engine turboprops and turbojets (i.e., business jets) have commercial, military, and private usages. For these aircraft, the representative spectrum was calculated using an equally weighted arithmetic average of all of the individual aircraft spectra. Reference 13 summarizes the aircraft included within each spectral class and their weighting towards the representative spectrum.

INM Version 6.0 contains 72 unique spectral classes: 31 classes for departure (classes 101-131); 34 classes for approach (classes 201-234); and 7 classes for level flyover (classes 301-307, applicable to helicopters only).

2.2.3 Maximum Noise Level Approximation

For several aircraft in the INM database, measured L_{ASmx} and L_{PNTSmx} NPD data do not exist, and they are approximated using empirical equations expressed as a function of distance and sound exposure. These equations were developed from a statistical analysis of NPD data for aircraft in which all four base noise-level metrics exist in the INM database. The equations are as follows:

For INM aircraft:
$$L_{ASmx} = L_{AE} - 7.19 - 7.73 \log_{10}[SLR_{pth}/1000]$$
$$L_{PNTSmx} = L_{EPN} + 1.12 - 9.34 \log_{10}[SLR_{pth}/1000] .$$

For NOISEMAP aircraft:
$$L_{ASmx} = L_{AE} - 7.84 - 6.06 \log_{10}[SLR_{pth}/1000]$$
$$L_{PNTSmx} = L_{EPN} + 2.51 - 5.84 \log_{10}[SLR_{pth}/1000] .$$

Where SLR_{pth} is the slant range (feet) to the closest-point-of-approach of an aircraft on a straight and level flight path.

2.2.4 C-Weighted Metric Approximation

The introduction of a spectral database into INM allows a user to calculate noise exposure in terms of C-weighted metrics. C-weighted metrics are calculated using a simplified adjustment procedure, consistent with FAR Part 36[10], as follows:
1. The aircraft spectrum is corrected back to the source.
2. The source spectrum is corrected to the ten standard INM distances assuming two conditions: an A-weighted spectrum and a C-weighted spectrum.
3. The two spectra are summed at each INM distance, and then arithmetically subtracted. This delta represents the difference between an A-weighted metric and a C-weighted metric at each distance.
4. The delta is applied to the appropriate A-weighted NPD values, resulting in a C-weighted NPD.

2.2.5 NPD Data Development Criteria

In the most general terms, criteria for development of NPD data for use by INM include the following:[14]

Acoustically soft ground under the measurement microphone, similar to the terrain around the microphone during aircraft noise certification tests.[10]

For L_{AE} and L_{EPN} values, an integrated adjustment procedure (involving time integration over the full spectral time history) as compared with a simplified adjustment procedure (involving the spectrum measured at the time of maximum noise level only) for airplanes where adequate field data are available.

Reference-day air attenuation coefficients as specified by SAE rather than standard-day conditions of 59 degrees Fahrenheit and 70 percent relative humidity used prior to INM Version 3.9.

L_{AE} and L_{EPN} values time-integrated over the upper 10 dB of the noise event as prescribed by FAA[10] and SAE[8]. (The time interval from t_1 to t_2 designates the time in seconds, from the beginning to the end of the integration period for the sound produced by an airplane. The duration $[t_2 - t_1]$ should be long enough to include all significant contributions to the total noise exposure. Sufficient accuracy is usually achieved by integration over the time interval during which the frequency-weighted sound level is within ten dB of its maximum value.)

L_{AE} and L_{EPN} values normalized to reference aircraft speed of 160 knots.

Noise levels specified as a function of power, usually corrected net thrust per engine.

The FAA position is to adhere closely to the above criteria both for the development and validation of the INM NPD data. Diligent compliance is needed to ensure confidence in having consistent and comparable aircraft NPD and performance data.

2.3   Flight Profile Calculation

INM 6.0 supports two kinds of flight profile input data: (1) an ordered set of profile points, and (2) an ordered set of procedure steps. The first section below discusses the structure of profile point data, and the remaining sections discuss how profile points are calculated from procedure steps.

2.3.1   Profile Point Input Data

An ordered set of profile points specifies a two-dimensional trajectory. For each point, the following data are given:

d	horizontal coordinate (feet) relative to an origin,
z	altitude of the aircraft above the airport (ft AFE),
v_T	aircraft true airspeed at the point (knots),
F_n/δ	corrected net thrust per engine (lb, %, or other units) at the point.

The origin is where the d-coordinate is equal to zero, and it depends on the kind of flight operation:

An approach origin is at the touchdown point, and d-values are <u>negative</u> during descent and positive during rollout on the runway.

A departure origin is at the start-roll point on a runway, and d-values are positive.

A touch-and-go origin is similar to an approach; the origin is where the aircraft touches down on the runway.

A circuit flight origin is similar to a departure; the origin is at the start-roll point.

An overflight origin is at the first point, and d-values are positive.

For all types of operations, d-values increase as an airplane flies along its profile.

Profile speed is the speed at the profile point; it is the magnitude of the aircraft velocity vector. It is the same as true airspeed with no wind, and the sections below refer to profile speed as true airspeed (TAS). Profile speed is approximately equal to ground speed, except when climbing or descending at steep angles.

The corrected net thrust per engine is in units of pounds, percent, or some other unit that is consistent with the noise curves. If the aircraft NPD curves are in percent, thrust-setting is a percentage of the aircraft static thrust value. In the sections that follow, F_n/δ is in pounds, but for some aircraft, the pounds are changed to percent before writing out the flight data.

When profile-point input data are used, INM does not correct for non-standard temperature and pressure. This means that the input values of F_n/δ are directly used in the noise tables.

2.3.2 Procedure Step Input Data

When a flight profile is specified in terms of procedure steps, INM processes the steps one at a time to calculate profile points, putting them in the same format as presented above.

Procedure steps are prescriptions for how to fly a profile. For example, the following set of procedure steps describes how to fly a jet departure profile:
1. Takeoff using 15-deg flaps and max-takeoff thrust.
2. Climb to 1000 ft AFE, using 15-deg flaps and max-takeoff thrust.
3. Accelerate to 175 kt CAS, while climbing at 2000 fpm and using 15-deg flaps and max-takeoff thrust.
4. Accelerate to 195 kt CAS, while climbing at 1000 fpm and using 5-deg flaps and cutting back to max-climb thrust.
5. Climb to 3000 ft AFE, using zero flaps and max-climb thrust.
6. Accelerate to 250 kt CAS, while climbing at 1000 fpm and using zero flaps and max-climb thrust.
7. Climb to 5500 ft AFE, using zero flaps and max-climb thrust.
8. Climb to 7500 ft AFE, using zero flaps and max-climb thrust.
9. Climb to 10000 ft AFE, using zero flaps and max-climb thrust.

Each procedure step is of a specific type (takeoff, climb, accelerate), and contains parameters relative to its type (15-deg flaps, 1000 ft AFE, 2000 fpm, max-climb thrust, etc.). The sections below show how each type of procedure step is processed to compute segment end-point values of altitude, speed, and thrust. Also, methods are presented to compute the segment horizontal distance, which is used to develop the d-coordinates for the set of profile points.

In general, one procedure step produces one profile point, but there are several exceptions. For example, a takeoff step produces two points (start-roll and takeoff rotation). Also, whenever there is a change in thrust setting (for example, going from max-takeoff to max-climb), an extra profile point is created so that thrust changes continuously over a small distance (1000 ft), rather than discontinuously at a point.

Sometimes, data from a current procedure step are combined with data from the previous step before a profile point can be computed. For example, a user inputs the starting descent altitude, speed, and angle. INM processes the next descent step to find its starting altitude, which is the ending altitude for the first step. In the development of procedure step methods that follow, these algorithmic details are not described. Instead, the production of profile points is discussed in terms of "initial" and "final" points that define a profile segment.

Before detailing the individual procedure step methods, the following two sections present equations that are used throughout.

2.3.3 Non-ISA Model for Atmospheric Ratios

This section presents the INM 6.0 equations for calculating atmospheric ratios of temperature, pressure, and density. "Non-ISA" means that the atmospheric ratios are different than those specified in the International Standard Atmosphere (ISA) model.[9]

The input parameters for the INM atmospheric ratio equations are:
> T   airport temperature (°F),
> P   airport pressure (inches-Hg) MSL,
> E   airport elevation (feet) MSL,
> A   aircraft altitude (feet) MSL.

Ambient temperature at the aircraft is calculated using input airport temperature and a constant temperature gradient above the airport, which is assumed to be the same as the ISA lapse rate of -0.003566°F per foot. INM calculates the absolute temperature ratio (theta) at aircraft altitude by the equation:
$$\theta = [459.67 + T - 0.003566 (A - E)] / 518.67 .$$
Theta is equal to the ISA temperature ratio when the input airport temperature T = 59°F and the airport elevation E = 0 feet MSL.

INM calculates the pressure ratio (delta) at aircraft altitude by the equation:
$$\delta = [(P / 29.92)^{1./5.256} - (0.003566 A / 518.67)]^{5.256} .$$
Delta is equal to the ISA pressure ratio when the input airport pressure P = 29.92 inches of mercury relative to mean sea level.

INM calculates the air density ratio (sigma) at aircraft altitude by the Ideal Gas Law:
$$\sigma = \delta / \theta .$$
Sigma is equal to the ISA air density ratio when both theta and delta are ISA values.

2.3.4 Corrected Net Thrust Per Engine For Departure

<u>Jet aircraft corrected net thrust per engine</u> is calculated by using a modified version of SAE-AIR-1845[8] equation (A1):

$$F_n/\delta = E + F v + G_A h + G_B h^2 + H T_C$$

where

F_n/δ corrected net thrust per engine (pounds),

v equivalent/calibrated airspeed (knots),

h pressure altitude (feet) MSL,

T_C temperature (°C) at the aircraft,

E, F, G_A, G_B, H

    regression coefficients that depend on power state (max-takeoff or max-climb power) and temperature state (below or above engine breakpoint temperature).

INM uses a quadratic estimate for the altitude term ($G_A h + G_B h^2$), rather than the linear estimate ($G h$) specified in SAE-AIR-1845.

Calibrated airspeed is assumed to equal equivalent airspeed (SAE-AIR-1845, page 26).

Pressure altitude is defined as ISA altitude at a given pressure ratio. INM calculates pressure altitude at the aircraft by the equation:

$$h = (518.67 / 0.003566)(1 - \delta^{1./5.256})$$

where

h pressure altitude (feet) MSL,

δ pressure ratio at aircraft altitude.

When the input airport pressure is 29.92 inches-Hg MSL, pressure altitude is equal to aircraft altitude ($h = A$).

The INM H-coefficient is in units of pounds per degree Celsius. Temperature at the aircraft in Fahrenheit is calculated by the equation:

$$T_F = T - 0.003566 (A - E)$$

and converted to Celsius by:

$$T_C = (5/9)(T_F - 32)$$

where

T_C temperature (°C) at the aircraft,

T_F temperature (°F) at the aircraft,

T airport temperature (°F),

E airport elevation (feet) MSL,

A aircraft altitude (feet) MSL.

INM models a jet engine by using four sets of coefficients: two sets for <u>max-takeoff</u> power and two sets for <u>max-climb</u> power. For a given power state, INM models the effect of jet engine breakpoint temperature by using coefficients $(E, F, G_A, G_B, H)_{low}$ for ambient temperatures below the breakpoint temperature and coefficients $(E, F, G_A, G_B, H)_{high}$ above breakpoint. INM calculates both $(F_n/\delta)_{low}$ and $(F_n/\delta)_{high}$ and then uses the smaller of the two values as the corrected net thrust for a given power state.

If the high-temperature coefficients do not exist in the database, INM calculates high-temperature corrected net thrust by the equation:[15]

$$(F_n/\delta)_{high} \;=\; F_{low}\,v \;+\; (E_{low} + H_{low}\,T_{BC})\,(1 - 0.003\,T_F) \,/\, (1 - 0.003\,T_{BF})$$

where

$(F_n/\delta)_{high}$	high-temperature corrected net thrust (pounds),
$E_{low}\ F_{low}\ H_{low}$	regression coefficients for the low-temperature equation,
v	calibrated airspeed (knots),
T_F	temperature (°F) at the aircraft,
T_{BC}, T_{BF}	breakpoint temperature, $T_{BC} = 30°C$, $T_{BF} = 86°F$.

Propeller-driven aircraft corrected net thrust per engine is calculated by using SAE-AIR-1845 equation (A4):

$$F_n/\delta \;=\; (325.87\ \eta\ P\ /\ v_T)\,/\,\delta$$

where

F_n/δ	corrected net thrust per engine (pounds),
η	propeller efficiency, which depends on the power state,
P	net power per engine (horsepower, MSL standard day), which depends on the power state (max-takeoff or max-climb),
v_T	true airspeed (knots),
δ	pressure ratio at aircraft altitude.

True airspeed is calculated by using SAE-AIR-1845 equation (A5):

$$v_T \;=\; v\,\sigma^{-\frac{1}{2}}$$

where

v_T	true airspeed (knots),
v	calibrated airspeed (knots),
σ	air density ratio at aircraft altitude.

Corrected net thrust per engine is used as an input parameter for calculating noise level using NPD curves, and it also appears in several SAE-AIR-1845 flight profile equations.

2.3.5 Takeoff Ground Roll Segment

For the takeoff ground roll segment, the initial and final values of aircraft altitude are given (the airport elevation), the initial and final values of speed and thrust are calculated, and the horizontal distance is calculated.

For jets, the corrected net thrust per engine $(F_n/\delta)_1$ at the start-roll point is calculated by using the departure thrust equation with $v_1 = 0$ knots. For props, the corrected net thrust per engine $(F_n/\delta)_1$ at the start-roll point is set equal to the corrected net thrust per engine $(F_n/\delta)_2$ at the takeoff rotation point.

For jets and props, the corrected net thrust per engine $(F_n/\delta)_2$ at the <u>takeoff rotation point</u> is calculated by using the departure thrust equations presented above. The calibrated airspeed at the rotation point, which is used in the thrust equation, is calculated by using SAE-AIR-1845 equation (A7):

$$v_2 = C_f W^{\frac{1}{2}}$$

where

   v_2 calibrated airspeed (kt) at takeoff rotation,
   C_f takeoff speed coefficient that depends on flaps setting,
   W departure profile weight (lb); weight is assumed to remain constant for the entire departure profile.

For jets or props, $(F_n/\delta)_1$ can be a user-input value. If so, $(F_n/\delta)_2$ is set equal to this value.

Takeoff <u>ground-roll distance</u> is calculated by using SAE-AIR-1845 equation (A6):

$$S_g = B_f \theta (W/\delta)^2 / [N (F_n/\delta)_2]$$

where

   S_g ground-roll distance (ft),
   B_f ground-roll coefficient, which depends on the flaps setting,
   θ temperature ratio at the airport elevation,
   W departure profile weight (lb),
   δ pressure ratio at the airport,
   N number of engines,
   $(F_n/\delta)_2$ corrected net thrust per engine (lb) at takeoff rotation.

The takeoff ground-roll distance is <u>corrected for headwind</u>, which may be different than the standard 8 knots, by using SAE-AIR-1845 equation (A16):

$$S_{gw} = S_g (v_2 - w)^2 / (v_2 - 8)^2$$

where

   S_{gw} ground-roll distance (ft) corrected for headwind,
   S_g ground-roll distance (ft) uncorrected,
   v_2 calibrated speed (kt) at takeoff rotation,
   w headwind (kt).

The takeoff ground-roll distance is also <u>corrected for runway gradient</u> by using the equations:

$$S_{gc} = S_{gw} a / (a - 32.17 G)$$
$$a = (v_2 \sigma^{-\frac{1}{2}})^2 / (2 S_{gw})$$
$$G = (E_2 - E_1) / L$$

where

   S_{gc} ground-roll distance (ft) corrected for headwind and runway gradient,
   S_{gw} ground-roll distance (ft) corrected for headwind,
   a average acceleration (ft/s^2) along the runway,
   v_2 calibrated speed (kt) at takeoff rotation,
   G runway gradient; G is positive when taking-off uphill,
   E_1,E_2 runway end elevations (ft) MSL,
   L runway length (ft).

In INM 6.0, the corrected ground-roll distance S_{gc} is divided into <u>six</u> equal-distance segments, and the start-roll speed v_1 is reset to 35 knots. The speed and thrust values at the six segment end points are calculated by linear interpolation on distance. The value of 35 knots at the first point is not a physical speed; instead, it is a coefficient that is used in the calculation of noise exposure behind start of takeoff roll. The noise exposure algorithm requires a non-zero segment speed (or else the exposure becomes infinite), and 35 knots is chosen so that noise exposure behind start of takeoff roll is commensurate with values obtained in previous versions of INM.

2.3.6 Touch-and-Go Power-On Ground Roll Segment

For that portion of a touch-and-go ground roll segment when an aircraft is accelerating to takeoff, the initial and final altitudes are given (the airport elevation), the initial calibrated speed v_{T1} is given (a user-defined value), and the final speed, initial and final thrusts, and horizontal distance are calculated.

The takeoff rotation speed v_{T2} is calculated by:
$$v_{T2} = C_f\, W^{\frac{1}{2}}\, \sigma^{-\frac{1}{2}}$$
where

$\quad C_f$ takeoff speed coefficient that depends on flaps setting,

$\quad W$ touch-and-go profile weight,

$\quad \sigma$ density ratio at the airport.

The thrusts $(F_n/\delta)_1$ and $(F_n/\delta)_2$ are calculated by using the departure thrust equations at the airport elevation and for calibrated speeds v_1 and v_2.

The power-on ground-roll distance is calculated by:
$$S_g = (v_{T2}^2 - v_{T1}^2) / (2\,a)$$
$$a = C_f^2\, N\, (F_n/\delta)_2 / (2\, B_f\, W/\delta)$$
where

$\quad S_g$ distance (ft) of that portion of the touch-and-go ground-roll that begins when accelerating power is applied and ends when takeoff rotation occurs,

$\quad v_{T1}$ initial true speed (kt),

$\quad v_{T2}$ final true speed (kt),

$\quad a$ average acceleration (ft/s^2) along the runway, which is assumed to be the same acceleration as available for takeoff,

$\quad C_f$ takeoff speed coefficient that depends on flaps setting,

$\quad N$ number of engines,

$\quad (F_n/\delta)_2$ corrected takeoff thrust (lb),

$\quad \delta$ pressure ratio at the airport,

$\quad B_f$ ground-roll coefficient that depends on flaps setting,

$\quad W$ touch-and-go profile weight (lb).

For the touch-and-go case, corrections for headwind, runway gradient, and segment subdivision are similar to those for the takeoff case.

2.3.7 Climb Segment

For a climb segment, the initial and final altitudes are given (A_1 is from the previous segment and A_2 is user input), the initial and final speeds are calculated using the final calibrated airspeed on the previous segment, the initial thrust $(F_n/\delta)_1$ is given from the previous segment, the final thrust is calculated, and the horizontal distance is calculated.

A climb segment is flown at constant calibrated airspeed v, climbing from altitude A_1 to altitude A_2. Even though a climb segment uses constant calibrated airspeed, the true airspeeds v_{T1} and v_{T2} at the segment end points are different because the air densities σ_1 and σ_2 are different. The speeds are calculated by:

$$v_{T1} = v \, \sigma_1^{-\frac{1}{2}}$$
$$v_{T2} = v \, \sigma_2^{-\frac{1}{2}} .$$

The <u>nominal</u> corrected net thrust per engine F_n/δ is usually calculated by using the departure thrust equations at the mid-point altitude $A_m = \frac{1}{2}(A_1 + A_2)$. Likewise, a nominal value of the pressure ratio δ is usually calculated at the mid-point altitude A_m.

The <u>final</u> corrected net thrust per engine $(F_n/\delta)_2$ is usually calculated by using the departure thrust equations at calibrated airspeed v and altitude A_2. However, there are three cases when this method is not used:

1. When a <u>"user-value" thrust</u> is specified, the nominal value of corrected net thrust per engine is set to the specified value, F_n/δ = user-value thrust. The nominal value of the pressure ratio δ is calculated at the mid-point altitude.

    The calculated initial corrected net thrust per engine $(F_n/\delta)_1$ is retained from the previous step, but the final corrected net thrust per engine is also set to the user-value thrust.

2. When <u>"user-cutback" thrust</u> is specified, the nominal value of corrected net thrust per engine is set to the specified value, F_n/δ = user-cutback thrust. The nominal value of the pressure ratio δ is calculated at the mid-point altitude.

    The climb segment is calculated and then it is broken into two sub-segments, both having the same climb angle. The first sub-segment is assigned a 1000-foot ground distance, and the corrected net thrust per engine at the end of 1000 feet is set equal to the user-cutback value. (If the original horizontal distance is less than 2000 feet, one half of the segment is used to cutback thrust.) The final thrust on the second sub-segment is also set equal to the user-cutback thrust. Thus, the second sub-segment is flown at constant thrust.

    Another 1000-foot sub-segment restores the thrust from the user-cutback value to the calculated value $(F_n/\delta)_2$ at altitude A_2, but this sub-segment is created in the next climb or acceleration segment.

3. When <u>engine-out "minimum-thrust"</u> is specified, the nominal value of corrected net thrust per engine F_n/δ is calculated by using the engine-out procedure below. The nominal value of the pressure ratio δ is set to the final value calculated at altitude A_2.

Two 1000-foot sub-segments are introduced in a manner similar to the user-cutback case. The constant engine-out reduced thrust used for the cutback sub-segment is calculated by:

$$F_n/\delta = (W/\delta_2) \{ [\sin(\tan^{-1}(G/100)) / K] + R_f \} / (N - 1)$$

where

F_n/δ	corrected net thrust per engine (lb) for an engine-out procedure,
W	departure profile weight (lb),
δ_2	pressure ratio at altitude A_2,
G	engine-out percentage climb gradient:
	G = 0% for aircraft with Automatic Thrust Restoration Systems; or if not,
	G = 1.2% for 2-engine aircraft,
	G = 1.5% for 3-engine aircraft,
	G = 1.7% for 4-engine aircraft,
K	speed-dependent constant:
	K = 1.01 when climb speed $\leq$ 200 kt, and K = 0.95 otherwise,
R_f	drag-over-lift coefficient that depends on the flaps setting,
N	number of engines (1 < N).

The average <u>climb angle</u> is calculated by using SAE-AIR-1845 equation (A8):

$$\gamma = \sin^{-1}(K [N (F_n/\delta)/(W/\delta) - R_f])$$

where

γ	average climb angle,
K	speed-dependent constant,
	K = 1.01 when climb speed $\leq$ 200 kt, and K = 0.95 otherwise,
N	number of engines,
F_n/δ	nominal value of corrected net thrust per engine (lb),
δ	nominal value of the pressure ratio,
W	departure profile weight (lb),
R_f	drag-over-lift coefficient that depends on the flaps setting.

The above method of setting the constant K is slightly different than specified in SAE-AIR-1845, where the initial climb segment uses K = 1.01, and climb segments after acceleration and flaps-retraction use K = 0.95. The INM method is more useful for handling flight profiles where the order of climb and acceleration segments is mixed.

The climb angle is <u>corrected for headwind</u> by using SAE-AIR-1845 equation (A17):

$$\gamma_w = \gamma (v - 8) / (v - w)$$

where

γ_w	average climb angle corrected for headwind,
γ	average climb angle, uncorrected
v	calibrated airspeed (kt) on the climb segment,
w	headwind (kt).

Finally, the <u>horizontal distance</u> for the climb segment is calculated by using SAE-AIR-1845 equation (A9):

$$S_c = (A_2 - A_1) / \tan(\gamma_w)$$

where

S_c horizontal distance (ft) for the climb segment,
    A_1 and A_2 are initial and final altitude (ft) MSL,
γ_w average climb angle corrected for headwind.

2.3.8 Acceleration Segment

For an acceleration segment, the initial altitude A_1, initial true airspeed v_{T1}, and initial thrust $(F_n/\delta)_1$ are given from the previous segment. The final calibrated airspeed v_2 and the average climb rate v_{Tz} are user inputs. The final altitude, final true airspeed, final thrust, and horizontal flying distance are calculated.

Altitude, speed, thrust, and distance are calculated by using an iterative method. The final altitude $A_2 = A_1 + 250$ feet is used for the first iteration, and then A_2 is recalculated until the absolute difference between the current and next iteration A_2 values is less than one foot.

The horizontal distance is calculated by using SAE-AIR-1845 equation (A10):

$$S_a = 0.95\, k\, (v_{T2}^2 - v_{T1}^2) / (G_m - G)$$

where

S_a current iteration horizontal distance (ft)
k constant $\frac{1}{2}(101.2686 / 60)^2 / 32.17$ (ft/kt^2),
v_{T1} input initial true airspeed (kt),
v_{T2} final true airspeed (kt) at current iteration σ_2: $v_{T2} = v_2\, \sigma_2^{-\frac{1}{2}}$,
v_2 input final calibrated airspeed (kt),
σ_2 air density ratio at current iteration final altitude A_2,
G_m maximum acceleration available (g's) for current iteration:
    $G_m = N\, (F_n/\delta) / (W/\delta) - R_f$
N number of engines,
F_n/δ average corrected net thrust per engine (lb) at the current iteration:
    $F_n/\delta = \frac{1}{2}[(F_n/\delta)_1 + (F_n/\delta)_2]$,
$(F_n/\delta)_1$ input initial corrected net thrust per engine (lb),
$(F_n/\delta)_2$ final corrected net thrust per engine (lb) at current iteration altitude A_2,
W departure profile weight (lb),
δ pressure ratio at current iteration mid-point altitude $\frac{1}{2}(A_1 + A_2)$,
R_f drag-over-lift coefficient that depends on the flaps setting,
G climb gradient for the current iteration value of v_{T2}:
    $G = v_{Tz} / [101.2686\ \frac{1}{2}(v_{T1} + v_{T2})]$,
v_{Tz} input climb rate (ft/min).

The next-iteration final altitude A_2' is calculated by using SAE-AIR-1845 equation (A11):

$$A_2' = A_1 + S_a\, G / 0.95 .$$

When $|A_2' - A_2| < 1$ foot, the current iteration values of final altitude A_2, final true airspeed v_{T2}, final corrected net thrust per engine $(F_n/\delta)_2$, and horizontal distance S_a are used for the acceleration segment.

If during the iteration process $(G_m - G) < 0.02$, the acceleration is considered to be too small to achieve the desired v_2 in a reasonable distance. INM issues a warning message and then limits the climb gradient to $G = G_m - 0.02$. In effect, the desired climb rate is reduced so that the airplane can maintain a minimum acceleration. If $G < 0.01$, INM issues an error message and stops computing the profile. This is because there is not enough thrust to both accelerate and climb, as required by the segment parameters.

The acceleration segment distance is <u>corrected for headwind</u> by using SAE-AIR-1845 equation (A18):

$$S_{aw} = S_a (v_T - w) / (v_T - 8)$$

where

S_{aw}	horizontal distance (ft) corrected for headwind,
S_a	horizontal distance (ft) for the acceleration segment, uncorrected,
v_T	average true airspeed (kt) on the segment: $v_T = \frac{1}{2}(v_{T1} + v_{T2})$,
w	headwind (kt).

2.3.9 Descent Segment

For a descent segment, the initial altitude, true airspeed, and thrust are given from the previous segment. The final altitude A_2, final calibrated airspeed v_2, and descent angle γ are user inputs. The final true airspeed, final thrust, and horizontal distance are calculated.

In INM, the initial altitude and speed appear to be user inputs; however, a descent segment is not actually calculated until the next segment is processed. This procedure is necessary so that an approach profile can start with a descent segment.

The final true airspeed is:

$$v_{T2} = v_2 \, \sigma_2^{-\frac{1}{2}}$$

where

v_2	input final calibrated airspeed,
σ_2	density ratio at altitude A_2.

The final corrected net thrust per engine is calculated by using by using SAE-AIR-1845 equation (A15):

$$(F_n/\delta)_2 = (W/\delta_2) [R_f - \sin(\gamma) / 1.03] / N$$

where

$(F_n/\delta)_2$	corrected net thrust per engine (lb) at altitude A_2,
W	profile weight (lb),
δ_2	pressure ratio at altitude A_2,
R_f	drag-over-lift coefficient that depends on flaps and gear setting,

γ average descent angle (a positive value),

N   number of engines.

The final corrected net thrust per engine is <u>corrected for headwind</u> by using SAE-AIR-1845 equation (A19):

$$(F_n/\delta)_{2w} = (F_n/\delta)_2 + 1.03 \ (W/\delta_2) \sin(\gamma) \ (w - 8) / (N \ v_2)$$

where

$(F_n/\delta)_{2w}$ corrected net thrust per engine (lb) for headwind w,

$(F_n/\delta)_2$ corrected net thrust per engine (lb) at altitude A_2,

W   profile weight (lb),

δ_2 pressure ratio at altitude A_2,

γ average descent angle (a positive value),

w   headwind (kt),

N   number of engines,

v_2 calibrated airspeed (kt) at altitude A_2.

The horizontal distance is calculated by:

$$S_d = (A_1 - A_2) / \tan(\gamma)$$

where

S_d horizontal distance (ft) for the descent segment,

A_1 initial altitude (ft) MSL,

A_2 final altitude (ft) MSL ($A_1 > A_2$),

γ average descent angle (a positive value).

2.3.10 Level Segment

For a level segment, the initial altitude, true airspeed, and thrust are given from the previous segment. The final altitude A_2, final calibrated airspeed v_2, and distance flown S_v are user inputs (the final altitude and speed must be the same as the initial values). The final thrust is calculated.

If the initial thrust is not the same as the final thrust (for example, the previous segment was a climb segment), then a 1000-ft transition segment is created so that the major portion of the level segment is flown at constant thrust.

The corrected net thrust per engine is calculated by using by using SAE-AIR-1845 equation (A15) with zero descent angle:

$$(F_n/\delta)_2 = (W/\delta) \ R_f / N$$

where

$(F_n/\delta)_2$ final corrected net thrust per engine (lb) at altitude $A_1 = A_2$,

W   profile weight (lb),

δ pressure ratio at altitude $A_1 = A_2$,

R_f drag-over-lift coefficient that depends on flaps and gear setting,

N   number of engines.

2.3.11 Cruise-Climb Segment

For a cruise-climb segment, the initial altitude, true airspeed, and thrust are given from the previous segment. The final altitude A_2, final calibrated airspeed v_2, and climb angle γ are user inputs (the initial and final calibrated airspeeds must be the same). The final true airspeed, final thrust, and horizontal distance are calculated. Cruise-climb thrust is less than "maximum-takeoff" or "maximum-climb" departure thrust.

The final corrected net thrust per engine is calculated by using by using SAE-AIR-1845 equation (A15) with an additive term for climb thrust:

$$(F_n/\delta)_2 = (W/\delta_2) [R_f + \sin(\gamma) / 0.95] / N$$

where

$(F_n/\delta)_2$ corrected net thrust per engine (lb) at altitude A_2,
W   profile weight (lb),
δ_2 pressure ratio at altitude A_2,
R_f drag-over-lift coefficient that depends on flaps and gear setting,
γ average climb angle (a positive value),
N   number of engines.

The horizontal distance is calculated by:

$$S_{cc} = (A_2 - A_1) / \tan(\gamma)$$

where

S_{cc} horizontal distance (ft) for the cruise-climb segment,
A_1, A_2 initial and final altitudes (ft) MSL ($A_1 < A_2$).

2.3.12 Landing Segment

For a landing segment, the initial and final altitudes are given (the airport elevation), the initial (landing) speed is calculated, the final roll-out true speed is calculated from user-input calibrated speed v_2, the initial (landing) thrust is calculated, the final thrust is calculated from a user-input percentage value P, and the ground-roll distance S_b is user input.

The landing calibrated airspeed is calculated by using SAE-AIR-1845 equation (A13):

$$v_1 = D_f W^{\frac{1}{2}}$$

where

v_1 calibrated airspeed (kt) just before landing,
v_{T1} landing true airspeed (kt), $v_{T1} = v_1 \sigma^{-\frac{1}{2}}$,
D_f landing coefficient that depends on the flaps and gear setting,
W   approach profile weight (lb); weight is assumed to remain constant for the entire approach profile.

The initial and final true speeds are calculated by:

$$v_{T1} = v_1 \sigma^{-\frac{1}{2}}$$
$$v_{T2} = v_2 \sigma^{-\frac{1}{2}}$$

where

σ density ratio at airport altitude.

The initial thrust $(F_n/\delta)_1$ is calculated using the descent thrust equation with the landing descent angle, landing calibrated airspeed v_1, and airport elevation (see Section 2.3.9).

The final thrust $(F_n/\delta)_2$ is calculated by:

$$(F_n/\delta)_2 \;=\; F_S\,(P/100)$$

where

$(F_n/\delta)_2$ corrected net thrust per engine (lb) at end of landing roll-out,
F_S static corrected net thrust per engine (an input parameter),
P percentage of thrust (an input parameter).

If the aircraft NPD curves are in percent, the value of "thrust" that is actually assigned to the flight segment is the percentage value P; it is used to directly access the noise tables.

2.3.13 Decelerate Segment

For a deceleration segment, the initial and final altitudes are given (the airport elevation), the initial speed is given from the previous step, and the final speed is calculated from user-input calibrated speed and density ratio. The initial thrust is given from the previous step, the final thrust is calculated from user-input percentage of thrust (see Section 2.3.12), and the ground-roll distance is user input.

2.4   Flight Path Calculation

An INM flight path is an ordered set of flight path segments. Each segment contains the following data:

x_1, y_1, z_1 starting coordinates for the segment (ft, ft, ft),
u_x, u_y, u_z unit vector directed along the segment,
L length of the segment (ft),
v_{T1} speed (kt) at the starting point, relative to x-y-z coordinates,
Δv change in speed (kt) along the segment: $\Delta v = v_{T2} - v_{T1}$,
$(F_n/\delta)_1$ corrected net thrust per engine (lb, %, or other) at the starting point,
ΔF change in corrected net thrust per engine (lb, %, or other) along the segment: $\Delta F = (F_n/\delta)_2 - (F_n/\delta)_1$.

The starting velocity vector (v_{T1} **u**) is directed along the segment, and the aircraft is assumed to continue to fly along the segment as speed and thrust change.   Segment true airspeed and length are used in the noise module to calculate the segment flying-time duration that a ground-based observer would experience.

Corrected net thrust per engine is in units of pounds, percent of static thrust, or other units, depending on the units defining the NPD curves.

Three-dimensional flight path segments are constructed by using ground track data and flight profile data, as discussed in the sections below.

2.4.1 Ground Track Processing

INM supports two kinds of ground tracks: (1) an ordered set of x,y points, and (2) an ordered set of vectoring commands (for example, fly straight 5.5 nmi, turn left 90° using radius 2.0 nmi).

INM transforms the vectoring commands into a set of x,y points. To do this, INM converts circular segments into multiple straight lines, processes approach tracks so that they line up with the runway, adds leader lines to approach tracks, and adds follower lines to departure tracks.

The details of circular arc conversion are discussed in Section 2.4.2 below.

When processing an approach vector track, INM starts the track at the origin and heads north. After all of the x-y points are calculated, the entire set of track points is rotated and translated to line-up with the approach end of the runway. INM makes the last track point coincide with the displaced approach threshold point on the runway. Then, a 200-nmi leader line is added to the beginning of the approach track (a new first point is added), so that the ground track is always longer than a profile.

When processing a departure vector track, INM makes the first track point coincide with the displaced takeoff threshold point on the runway. A 200-nmi follower line is added to the end of a departure or overflight track, so that the ground track is always longer than a profile. Touch-and-go ground tracks are not extended.

2.4.2 Circular Arc Conversion

INM approximates a circular-arc ground track with two or more straight-line segments. The method of Reference 16 is used. First, the number of sub-arcs contained in the circular arc is computed:

$$N = int(1 + A/60)$$

where

N	number of sub-arcs,
A	given circular arc (degrees),
int(x)	function that returns the integer part of x.

Then, the angular size of each sub-arc is computed:

$$\alpha = A / N .$$

For each sub-arc, three x-y points are computed. These three points define two line segments. The first point is at the start of the sub-arc, and the third point is at the end of the sub-arc. The second point is half-way along the sub-arc, but not located on it. The distance from the center of the sub-arc to the second point, instead of being the arc radius, is computed by:

$$r_2 = r \left[\cos\tfrac{1}{2}\alpha + (\tfrac{1}{4}\alpha^2 - \sin^2\tfrac{1}{2}\alpha)^{\frac{1}{2}} \right]$$

where

      r_2 distance from the center of the sub-arc to the second point,

      r   radius of the sub-arc,

      α magnitude of the sub-arc (radians).

This method ensures that a line segment replaces not more than 30 degrees of turn angle. Also, the sum of the lengths of the line segments equals the distance along the arc, so that the flying time along the line segments is the same as the time that would be flown along the circular arc.

2.4.3 3-D Flight Path Construction

A three-dimensional flight path is constructed by merging a two-dimensional profile (a set of distance vs. altitude points) with a two-dimensional ground track (a set of x-y points). Wherever there is a track point, a z-value is computed by interpolating between two points on the profile. Wherever there is a profile point, x-y values are computed on the ground-track segment under the profile point. The result of this construction is an ordered set of x,y,z points and associated speed and thrust data that describe the flight path.

When a track point lies between two profile points, a linear interpolation method is used to calculate the altitude, speed, and thrust:

$$z = z_1 + f(z_2 - z_1)$$
$$v_T = v_{T1} + f(v_{T2} - v_{T1})$$
$$F_n/\delta = (F_n/\delta)_1 + f[(F_n/\delta)_2 - (F_n/\delta)_1]$$

where

      z   altitude above the airport at the interpolated point,

      f   fraction of the distance from profile point 1 to the interpolated point divided by the distance from profile point 1 to point 2,

      z_1, z_2 initial and final profile altitudes,

      v_T speed at the interpolated point,

      v_{T1}, v_{T2} initial and final profile speeds,

      F_n/δ corrected net thrust per engine at the interpolated point,

      $(F_n/\delta)_1, (F_n/\delta)_2$

            initial and final profile thrust.

2.4.4 Displaced Thresholds and Threshold Crossing Heights

A departure flight path starts at a given distance from the departure end of the runway:

$$D = D_{dep} + \Delta_{trk}$$

where

      D   start-roll distance (ft) from the end of the runway,

      D_{dep} displaced departure threshold (ft) for the runway (user input),

      Δ_{trk} delta distance (ft) for the departure ground track (user input).

An approach or touch-and-go flight touches down on the runway a given distance from the approach end of the runway:

$$D = D_{app} + \Delta_{trk} + h_{tc} |d_{-1}| / z_{-1}$$

where

D	touch-down distance (ft) from the end of the runway,
D_{app}	displaced approach threshold (ft) for the runway (user input),
Δ_{trk}	delta distance (ft) for the approach ground track (user input),
h_{tc}	threshold crossing height (ft) for the runway (user input),
d_{-1}	coordinate value (ft) of the profile point immediately before the touch-down point (it is a negative number),
z_{-1}	altitude (ft AFE) of the profile point immediately before the touch-down point (the touch-down point has coordinates: $d_o = 0$, $z_o = 0$).

2.4.5 Touch-and-Go and Circuit Flight Path Methods

INM uses special processing to construct touch-and-go and circuit flight paths.

A user-defined <u>touch-and-go profile</u> starts in level flight at airport pattern altitude, descends, touches down on the runway, rolls out, takes off, climbs, and ends somewhere after leveling off at pattern altitude. After associating a touch-and-go profile with a touch-and-go track, but before calculating flight path points, INM reorders and modifies the set of profile points so that the profile starts and ends at the touchdown point. While reordering the points, INM inserts an extra level segment in the downwind portion of the profile (between the last departure point and first approach point), so that the profile distance is the same as the track distance. Also, a final touchdown point is added at the end. When finished, the new profile starts at touchdown, ends at touchdown, and has horizontal coordinate distance equal to the touch-and-go ground track distance.

A user-defined <u>circuit profile</u> starts on the runway as a standard departure, takes off, climbs to pattern altitude, levels out, descends from pattern altitude, lands, and decelerates to taxi speed. After associating a circuit profile with a touch-and-go track (there are no circuit tracks), INM inserts an extra level segment in the downwind portion of the profile, so that the profile distance is the same as the track distance. The place where the extra segment is inserted is determined by the "level-stretch" procedure step, which is provided by the user.

After modifying a touch-and-go or circuit profile, INM merges the new profile points and the ground track points to compute a three-dimensional flight path.

2.4.6 Segments Too Short and Too Long

After INM constructs the ordered set of flight path points, they are processed to remove points that are too close together. If two (x, y, z) points are closer than 10 feet, and if the speed and thrust data are the same, one of the points is removed from the set of points.

The last step in constructing a flight path is to insert points into segments that are too long. A path segment is subdivided if its length multiplied by the change in speed is greater than 100,000 foot-knots. The number of sub-segments is calculated by:

$$N = \text{int}\left(1 + [(v_{T2} - v_{T1}) L \, 10^{-5}]^{\frac{1}{2}}\right)$$

where

N	number of equal-distance sub-segments,
int(x)	function that returns the integer part of a number x,
v_{T1}	initial speed (knot),
v_{T2}	final speed (knot),
L	length of the segment (feet).

If the flight path segment is subdivided, the speed and thrust values at the end points of the equal-distance sub-segments are linearly interpolated by using the initial and final end-point values.

3   ACOUSTIC COMPUTATION METHODOLOGY

Chapter 3 describes the acoustic computation methodology employed by INM 6.0. The starting point for these calculations is a noise database that provides aircraft source noise characteristics. The INM noise database includes noise-power-distance (NPD) data (see Section 2.2.1) and aircraft spectral class data (see Section 2.2.2). The following sections describe the generation of noise-level and time-above metrics at a single observer, or at an evenly-spaced regular grid of observers, including the regular grid of observers that is used in the development of the recursively-subdivided irregular grid for noise contour analysis. Much of the discussion presented herein is based on information given in Reference 8.

Chapter 3 contains the following sections:

Section 3.1	Gives an overview of the INM reference data.
Section 3.2	Describes the computation of the flight path segment geometric and physical parameters.
Section 3.3	Describes the flight path segment noise interpolation and extrapolation process.
Section 3.4	Describes the atmospheric absorption adjustment of NPD data, based on user-supplied local temperature and relative humidity.
Section 3.5	Describes a temperature/pressure dependent NPD acoustic impedance adjustment.
Section 3.6	Describes the computation of the flight-segment noise fraction adjustment for exposure-based noise level metrics.
Section 3.7	Describes the computation of the aircraft speed duration adjustment for exposure-based noise level metrics.
Section 3.8	Describes the computation of the lateral attenuation adjustment.
Section 3.9	Describes the ground-based directivity adjustment behind the start-of-takeoff roll, and the computations of metrics for runup operations.
Section 3.10	Describes how the flight-segment computations of Sections 3.2 through 3.9 are used to compute the exposure-based noise level metrics.
Section 3.11	Describes the computation of maximum noise level metrics.
Section 3.12	Describes the computation of time-above metrics.
Section 3.13	Explains the difference between single-metric and multi-metric contour analyses.

Figure 3-1 Graphically summarizes the acoustic computation process employed in INM 6.0.

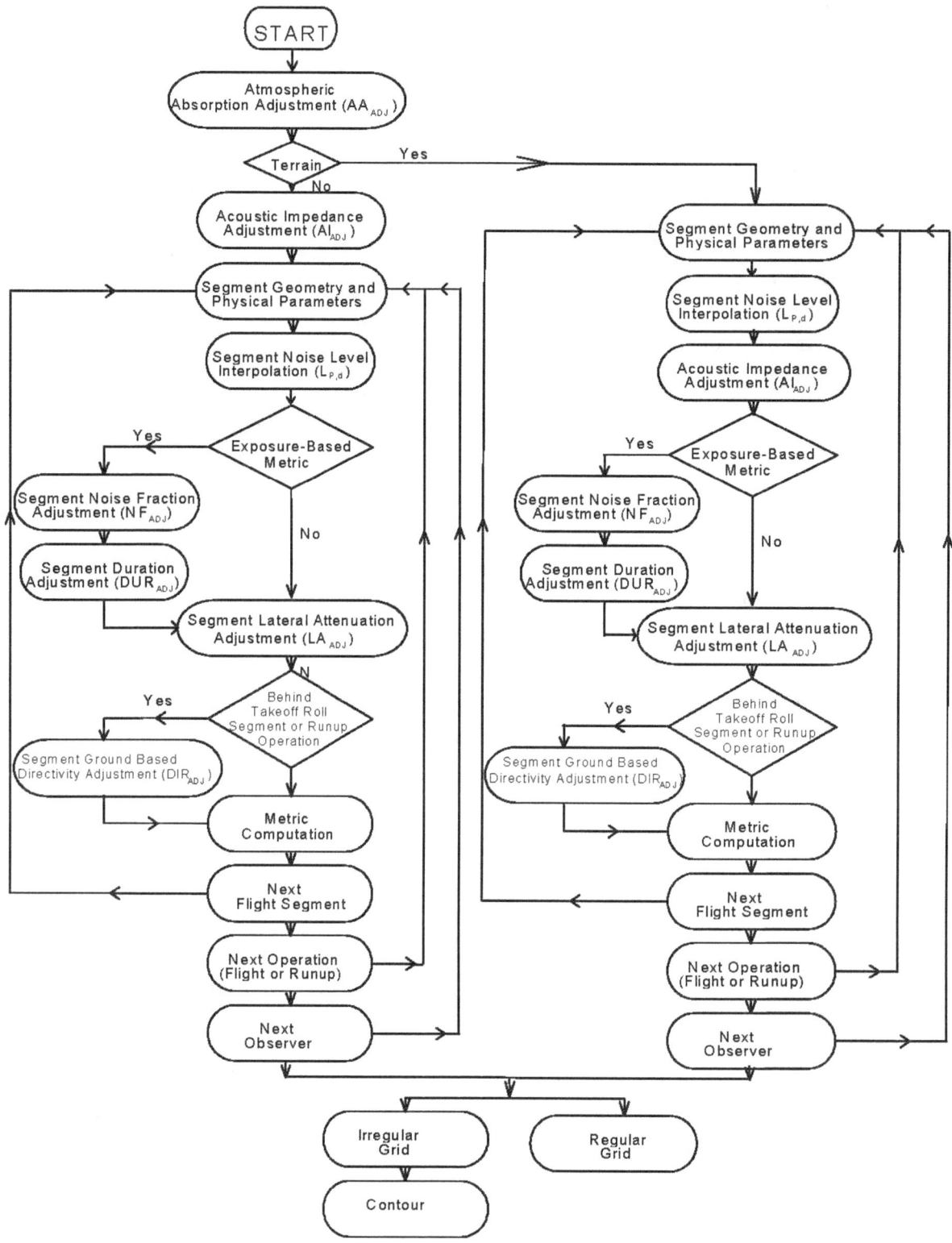

Figure 3-1: INM 6.0 Acoustic Computation Process

3.1   INM Reference Data

The input data for all acoustic calculations in the INM include both the reference Noise Power Distance (NPD) data sets (Section 2.2.1) and Spectral Class data sets (Section 2.2.2).

Normal NPD data consists of two or more noise curves. The engine "power" in the NPD relations serves as a simple surrogate for the state of the aircraft and reflects the changes in the noise source as the aircraft/engine state changes. Examples of "power" include corrected net thrust, percent-corrected net thrust, and RPM. Distance-based noise levels are approximated by correcting the noise levels to the following ten distances: 200, 400, 630, 1000, 2000, 4000, 6300, 10000, 16000, and 25000 feet. The guidelines for these corrections are provided in SAE-AIR-1845[8].

Spectral data provide a way of enhancing the propagation algorithms of the INM acoustics model by assigning a nominal "spectral shape" to an NPD curve relationship. To implement these improvements, it is important to verify that the spectral shape assigned is representative of the true source spectra used to create the NPD curves in accordance with SAE-AIR-1845. Spectral classes are stored in INM, corrected to 1000 feet using the SAE-AIR-1845 atmosphere and normalized to 70 dB at 1000 Hz.

INM provides separate NPD/Spectral class data sets for approach and departure conditions to model additional changes in aircraft state not captured by power setting alone.

3.2   Flight Path Segment Parameters

As a prerequisite to noise level computations, INM computes several geometric and physical parameters associated with an aircraft flight path. Section 3.2 describes the computation of these parameters.

Computation of the following flight-segment geometric parameters is discussed in Section 3.2.1: (1) the closest point of approach on the flight-path segment, or the extended flight-path segment, to the observer; and (2) the slant range from the observer location to the closest point of approach.

Computation of the following flight-segment geometric and physical parameters is discussed in Section 3.2.2: (1) the speed along the flight-path segment; (2) the altitude associated with the flight-path segment; (3) the over-ground, sideline distance from the observer location to the ground-projection of the closest point of approach; and (4) the engine power associated with the flight-path segment.

Figures 3-2 through 3-4 present, respectively, the observer/flight-segment geometry for the three general INM cases: (1) the observer is behind the flight-path segment; (2) the observer is astride the flight-path segment; and (3) the observer is ahead of the flight-path segment.

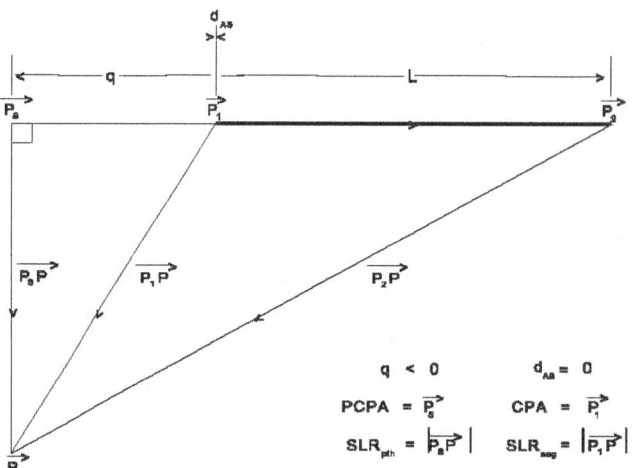

Figure 3-2 Flight–Segment Geometry when an Observer is Behind a Segment

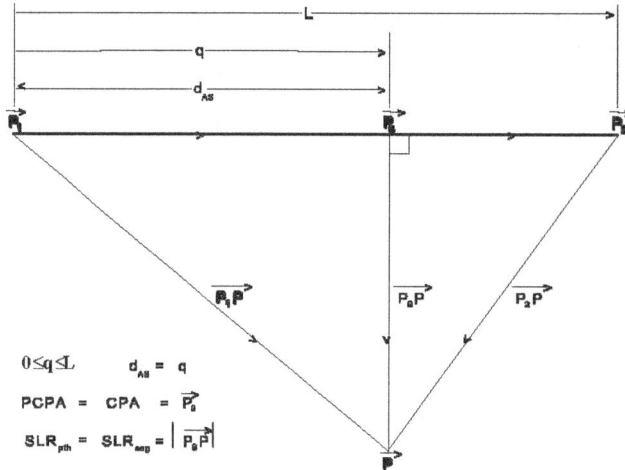

Figure 3-3 Flight–Segment Geometry when an Observer is Astride a Segment

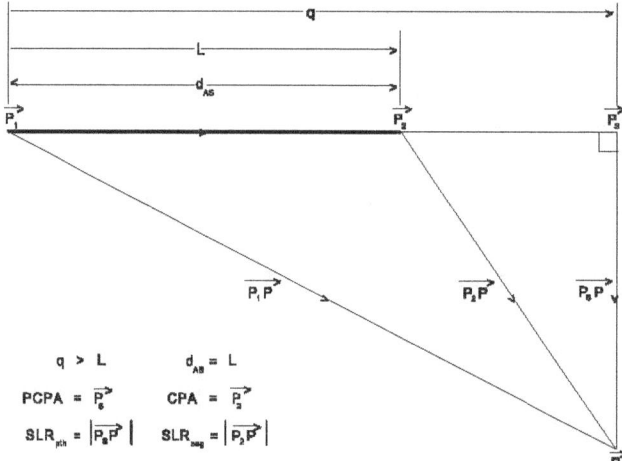

Figure 3-4 Flight-Segment Geometry when an Observer is Ahead of a Segment

The variables shown in these figures are defined as follows:

P   observer point.

P_1 start-point of the flight-path segment.

P_2 end-point of the flight-path segment.

P_S PCPA, the point on the flight-path segment, or the extended flight-path segment, which is the perpendicular closest point of approach to the observer, as defined in detail in Section 3.2.1, below. The specific definition depends on the position of the observer relative to the flight-path segment.

P_1P_2 vector from the start of the flight-path segment to the end of the flight-path segment. It has a minimum length of 10 feet.

P_1P vector from the start of the flight-path segment to the observer. It has a minimum length of 1 foot.

P_2P vector from the end of the flight-path segment to the observer. It has a minimum length of 1 foot.

P_SP perpendicular vector from the observer to PCPA on the flight-path segment, or the extended flight-path segment, as defined in detail in Section 3.2.1. It has a minimum length of 1 foot.

SLR_{pth} $|P_SP|$, the length of the perpendicular vector from the observer to PCPA on the flight-path segment, or the extended flight-path segment, as defined in detail in Section 3.2.1. It has a minimum value of 1 foot.

L   length of the flight-path segment. It has a minimum value of 10 feet.

CPA   point on the flight-path segment, not the extended flight-path segment, which is the closest point of approach to the observer, as defined in detail in Section 3.2.1, below. The specific definition depends on the position of the observer relative to the flight-path segment.

SLR_{seg} length of the vector from the observer to CPA on the flight-path segment, not the extended flight-path segment, as defined in detail in Section 3.2.1. It has a minimum value of 1 foot.

q   relative distance along the flight-path segment, or the extended flight-path segment, from P_1 to P_S (feet). The value of q is used to determine the position of the observer relative to the flight-path segment, as shown in Table 3-1.

d_{AS} distance along the flight-path segment from the start of the segment at $\mathbf{P}_1$, to CPA. Depending on the value of q, i.e., the relative geometry between the observer and the flight-path segment, d_{AS} takes on the values shown in Table 3-1.

Table 3-1 Position of the Observer Relative to the Flight-Path Segment

Value of q	Value of d_{AS}	Position of observer relative to flight path segment
$q < 0$	0	Observer is behind segment
$0 \le q \le L$	q	Observer is astride segment
$q > L$	L	Observer is ahead of segment

3.2.1 Closest Point of Approach and Slant Range

The closest point of approach and slant range parameters are fundamental parameters to INM 6.0 computations. The slant range is used for noise-level interpolation of the NPD data (see Section 3.3). In addition, their computation is a prerequisite to the noise fraction algorithm used for exposure-based metrics (see Section 3.6).

The slant range from the observer location to the closest point of approach on the flight path, SLR_{pth}, is defined as the distance from the perpendicular closest point of approach (PCPA), on the flight-path segment, or the extended flight-path segment, to the observer. The specific definition of PCPA depends upon the position of the observer location relative to the flight-path segment. If the observer is behind or ahead of the flight-path segment, then PCPA is the intersection point of the perpendicular from the observer to the extended segment. If the observer is astride the flight-path segment, then PCPA is the intersection point of the perpendicular from the observer to the segment.

The exceptions to the above definition for slant range occur: (1) when the observer is behind a takeoff ground-roll segment (see Section 3.9); (2) for runup operations; and (3) when performing computations involving L_{ASmx}, L_{PNTSmx}, or time-above metrics. In these cases, the slant range, designated SLR_{seg}, is defined as the distance from the observer location to the closest point of approach on the flight-path segment, designated CPA, not the extended flight-path segment. The specific definition of CPA depends on the position of the observer location relative to the flight-path segment. If the observer is behind the flight-path segment, CPA is the start point of the segment. If the observer is astride the flight-path segment, CPA is equivalent to PCPA. If the observer is ahead of the flight-path segment, CPA is the end point of the flight-path segment.

3.2.2 Speed, Altitude, Distance, and Power

Computations of the following four parameters, associated with each flight-path segment, are described: (1) the speed at CPA; (2) the altitude at CPA; (3) the horizontal sideline distance from the observer location to the vertical projection of CPA; and (4) the engine power setting at CPA.

The aircraft speed, AS_{seg}, at CPA is computed via linear interpolation as follows:

$$AS_{seg} = AS_{P1} + [d_{AS} / L] \Delta AS \qquad \text{(knots)}$$

where

AS_{P1} speed at the start of the flight-path segment (knots),

d_{AS} defined in Section 3.2,

L defined in Section 3.2,

ΔAS change in speed along the flight-path segment (knots).

AS_{seg} is used to compute the duration adjustment for exposure-based noise-level metrics as discussed in Section 3.7.

The altitude, d_{seg}, at CPA is computed via linear interpolation:

$$d_{seg} = [\mathbf{P}_1]_z + d_{AS} [(\mathbf{P}_1\mathbf{P}_2)_z / L] + h_{terr} - h_{aprt} \qquad \text{(feet)}$$

where

$[\mathbf{P}_1]_z$ altitude at the start of the flight path segment, given by the z-component of the vector from the origin of coordinates to the start of the flight-path segment (feet above airport elevation),

d_{AS} defined in Section 3.2,

$(\mathbf{P}_1\mathbf{P}_2)_z$ change in altitude along the flight-path segment (feet),

L defined in Section 3.2,

h_{terr} terrain elevation (feet MSL); when the terrain option is not invoked, $h_{terr} = h_{aprt}$,

h_{aprt} airport elevation (feet MSL).

The sideline distance from the flight-path segment to the observer, l_{seg}, defined as the distance in the horizontal plane from the observer location on the ground to the vertical projection of CPA, is computed as follows:

$$l_{seg} = (SLR_{seg}^2 - d_{seg}^2)^{\frac{1}{2}}$$

where

SLR_{seg} defined in Section 3.2,

d_{seg} as computed above.

The sideline distance, l_{seg}, is used to compute the ground-to-ground component of the lateral attenuation adjustment as discussed in Section 3.8.

The engine power setting,* P_{seg}, at CPA is computed via linear interpolation:

$$P_{seg} = P_{P1} + [d_{AS} / L] \Delta P$$

where

P_{P1} engine power at the start of the flight-path segment,

d_{AS} defined in Section 3.2,

L defined in Section 3.2,

ΔP change in power along the flight-path segment.

---

* Engine power setting, also known as thrust-setting, is expressed on a per engine basis in a variety of units, including pounds, percent, engine-pressure-ratio (EPR), as well as other units. The specific unit designation can be found in the THRSET_TYP field in the *NOIS_GRP.DBF* database file.

P_{seg} is used in performing noise level interpolation as discussed in Section 3.3.

3.3   Noise Level Interpolation ($L_{P,d}$)

The NPD data are used to either interpolate or extrapolate an associated noise-level value. The interpolation/extrapolation is a piece-wise linear process between the engine power setting and the base-10 logarithm of the distance.

Interpolation or extrapolation of NPD data for departure operations is performed using the NPD curves designated as departure curves. Similarly, interpolation or extrapolation of NPD data for approach operations, with one exception, is performed using the NPD curves designated as approach curves. The one exception occurs for the thrust reverse segment after aircraft touchdown. For this segment interpolation/extrapolation is performed using the departure NPD curves because of the higher noise levels associated with both departure and reverse thrust.

For each aircraft flight operation, NPD data are available for the four fundamental noise-level metrics, L_{AE}, L_{EPN}, L_{ASmx}, and L_{PNTSmx}. The appropriate metric is selected for interpolation or extrapolation based upon the user-specified noise metric, or family of metrics to be computed at the observer. The specific distance and power value used in the interpolation/extrapolation process is dependent on the type of base metric selected. Section 3.2.1 and 3.2.2 discuss the distance and power values for exposure-based noise-level metrics and maximum noise-level metrics, respectively.

Following is a generalized description of the noise interpolation for an engine power P* and distance d. For this interpolation, the engine power is bounded by NPD curves with engine power P_1 and P_2. Within these NPD curves, the distance d is bounded by the NPD distances of d_1 and d_2. For extrapolation, P_1 and P_2 and d_1 and d_2 are chosen to be the core database values "closest" to the desired power P or distance d.

The noise level at engine power, P_1, and distance, d, is given by:

$$L_{P1,d} = L_{P1,d1} + (L_{P1,d2} - L_{P1,d1}) (\log_{10} d - \log_{10} d_1) / (\log_{10} d_2 - \log_{10} d_1) \qquad \text{(dB)}$$

where

P_1, P_2 engine power values for which noise data are available in the NPD database,
d_1, d_2 distance values for which noise data are available in the NPD database,
$L_{P1,d1}$ noise level at power P_1 and distance d_1 (dB),
$L_{P2,d1}$ noise level at power P_2 and distance d_1 (dB),
$L_{P1,d2}$ noise level at power P_1 and distance d_2 (dB),
$L_{P2,d2}$ noise level at power P_2 and distance d_2 (dB).

---

* Several of the NOISEMAP aircraft, which were included in the INM database beginning with Version 5.1, contain NPD data for afterburner operations (NOISEMAP equivalent of "FIXED" interpolation). These data are identified in the CURVE_TYPE field in the *NPD_CURV.DBF* database file with an "X" for Afterburner, as compared to an "A" for Approach or "D" for Depart. If a particular flight path segment is identified as an afterburner segment, interpolation or extrapolation is only performed with regard to distance, not power.

The noise level at engine power P_2 and distance d is given by:

$$L_{P2,d} = L_{P2,d1} + (L_{P2,d2} - L_{P2,d1}) (\log_{10} d - \log_{10} d_1) / (\log_{10} d_2 - \log_{10} d_1) \qquad \text{(dB)}$$

Finally, the interpolated/extrapolated noise level at engine power P and distance d is given by:

$$L_{P,d} = L_{P1,d} + (L_{P2,d} - L_{P1,d}) (P - P_1) / (P_2 - P_1) \qquad \text{(dB)}$$

The above methodology is utilized when: (1) the engine power and/or distance associated with the observer/segment pair lies between existing values in the NPD data (i.e., interpolation); (2) the power and/or distance associated with the observer/segment pair is larger than existing values in the NPD data (i.e., extrapolation); or (3) the power associated with the observer/segment pair is smaller than existing values in the NPD data (i.e., extrapolation). When noise levels are extrapolated to power settings below those represented by the NPD curves, the extrapolation is limited to 5 dB below the lowest noise curve.

When the distance associated with the observer/segment pair is smaller than the smallest distance in the NPD data (i.e., 200 ft) a special case applies. This special case is discussed separately for exposure-based noise-level metrics (Section 3.3.1) and maximum noise-level metrics (Section 3.3.2).

3.3.1 Exposure-Based Noise Level Metrics

The general noise interpolation/extrapolation process described in Section 3.3 is applicable for the four fundamental noise-level metrics, L_{AE}, L_{EPN}, L_{ASmx}, and L_{PNTSmx}. However, the specific engine power and distance value used in the interpolation/extrapolation process is different for exposure-based noise-level metrics as compared with maximum noise-level metrics.

If the end points of a flight-path segment are defined by $\mathbf{P}_1$ at the start of the segment, and $\mathbf{P}_2$ at the end of the segment, then the exposure-based noise level, either L_{AE} or L_{EPN} interpolated or extrapolated for an observer/segment pair, is given by:

$$L_{P,d} = \begin{cases} L_{Pseg,d=SLRpth} & \text{observer behind or ahead of segment} \\ L_{Pseg,d=SLRseg} & \text{observer astride segment} \end{cases}$$

where

$L_{Pseg,d=SLRpth}$ Interpolated noise level (dB) based upon engine power associated with the flight-path segment, P_{seg}, as defined in Section 3.2.2, and the distance to PCPA on the extended flight-path segment, as defined in Section 3.2.1;

$L_{Pseg,d=SLRseg}$ Interpolated noise level (dB) based upon engine power associated with the flight path segment, P_{seg}, and the distance to CPA=PCPA on the flight-path segment.

For the special case in which SLR_{pth} or SLR_{seg} is smaller than 200 feet, i.e., the smallest value in the distance portion of the NPD data, cylindrical divergence (i.e., line-source) is assumed and a $10 \log_{10}[d_1/d_2]$ relationship is used for the L_{AE}-based and L_{EPN}-based noise-level metrics. For example, if L_{AE} at 200 feet and for a given power setting in the NPD data is 95.6 dB, the extrapolated L_{AE} at 100 feet and at the same power setting is 98.6 dB (95.6 + 10 $\log_{10}$[200/100]).

3.3.2 Maximum Noise Level Metrics

The general noise interpolation/extrapolation process described in Section 3.3 is applicable for the four fundamental noise-level metrics, L_{AE}, L_{EPN}, L_{ASmx}, and L_{PNTSmx}. However, the specific distance and power value used in the interpolation/extrapolation process is different for maximum noise-level metrics as compared with exposure-based metrics.

If the end points of a flight-path segment are defined by $\mathbf{P}_1$ at the start of the segment, and $\mathbf{P}_2$ at the end of the segment, then the maximum noise level, either L_{ASmx} or L_{PNTSmx}, as appropriate, interpolated/extrapolated for an observer/segment pair, is given by:

$$L_{P,d} = \begin{cases} \text{Max}[\ L_{P,d,START},\ L_{P,d,END}\ ] & \text{observer behind/ahead of segment} \\ \text{Max}[\ L_{P,d,START},\ L_{P,d,PCPA},\ L_{P,d,END}\ ] & \text{observer astride segment} \end{cases}$$

where

Max[ ]	Function that returns the maximum of two or three noise level values,
$L_{P,d,START}$	Interpolated noise level (dB) based upon the distance and engine power values associated with the start of the flight-path segment,
$L_{P,d,END}$	Interpolated noise level (dB) based upon the distance and engine power values associated with the end of the flight-path segment,
$L_{P,d,PCPA}$	Interpolated noise level (dB) based upon the distance and engine power values associated with PCPA = CPA on the flight path segment.

As with exposure-based metrics, a special case applies for maximum noise level metrics when the distance is smaller than 200 feet. For the L_{ASmx}-based and L_{PNTSmx}-based noise metrics, spherical divergence (i.e., a point-source) is assumed and a 20 $\log_{10}$[d_1/d_2] relationship is used. For example, if L_{ASmx} at 200 feet and for given power setting in the NPD database is 95.6 dB, then the extrapolated L_{ASmx} at 100 feet at the same power setting is 95.6 + 20 $\log_{10}$[200/100] = 101.6 dB.

3.4 Atmospheric Absorption Adjustment (AA_{ADJ})

The introduction of a spectral database into INM allows a user to take into account atmospheric absorption due to the effects of temperature and relative humidity on an airport-specific basis. Sound levels tend to be lower in low humidity environments as compared to high humidity ones due to the increased atmospheric absorption associated with the lower humidity.[7]

The spectral data in INM has been corrected to reference day conditions, using the SAE AIR-1845 standard atmosphere, at a distance of 305 m. The following steps, which are consistent with the simplified procedure of FAR Part 36[10], are used to correct the data to the user-specified temperature and relative humidity:

1. The aircraft spectrum is A-weighted (or C-weighted, as appropriate) and corrected back to the source (effectively removing the SAE AIR-1845 atmosphere).
2. The source spectrum is then corrected to the 10 standard INM distances assuming two conditions: a user-supplied atmosphere based on SAE ARP-866A[7] and the SAE AIR-1845[8] atmosphere.
3. The two spectra are summed over the 24 one-third octave bands at each INM distance, and the two decibel values are subtracted.

The decibel difference, computed at each distance, is an adjustment that is applied to the INM NPD data to take into account the user-defined temperature and humidity.

For example, the following illustrates the derivation of the atmospheric absorption correction for INM departure spectral class #103, using the absorption associated with a temperature of 59°F (15°C) and relative humidity equal to 70%. First, the values for spectral class #103 are presented below. This is a flat (un-weighted) spectrum, corrected using SAE-AIR-1845 to 305 m and normalized to 70 dB at 1000 Hz.

INM Departure Class #103

Frequency (Hz)	50	63	80	100	125	160	200	250	315	400	500	630
Normalized Level (dB)	56.7	66.1	70.1	72.8	76.6	73.0	74.5	77.0	75.3	72.2	72.2	71.2
Frequency (Hz)	800	1000	1250	1600	2000	2500	3150	4000	5000	6300	8000	10000
Normalized Level (dB)	70.2	70.0	69.6	71.1	70.6	67.1	63.4	63.5	58.2	51.5	42.3	37.7

The following data represent the A-weighted spectral class data corrected to the source (a theoretical distance of 0 feet) for atmospheric absorption.

Step 1: A-weighted Spectral Class Corrected to Source

Frequency (Hz)	50	63	80	100	125	160	200	250	315	400	500	630
Normalized Level (dB)	26.6	40.0	47.7	53.9	60.7	59.9	64.0	68.8	69.3	68.1	69.9	70.4
Frequency (Hz)	800	1000	1250	1600	2000	2500	3150	4000	5000	6300	8000	10000
Normalized Level (dB)	70.8	71.8	72.5	75.1	75.8	73.6	71.6	74.0	69.7	67.4	63.2	65.2

The following data represent the "source" spectral class corrected to a distance of 1000 feet.

Step 2a: Source Spectrum Corrected to Distance of 1000 Feet using SAE-866A

Frequency (Hz)	50	63	80	100	125	160	200	250	315	400	500	630
Normalized Level (dB)	26.5	39.9	47.6	53.8	60.5	59.7	63.7	68.4	68.9	67.5	69.2	69.5
Frequency (Hz)	800	1000	1250	1600	2000	2500	3150	4000	5000	6300	8000	10000
Normalized Level (dB)	69.6	70.3	70.7	72.7	72.8	69.6	66.1	66.4	60.6	54.6	44.6	37.8

Step 2b: Source Spectrum Corrected to Distance of 1000 Feet using SAE-AIR-1845

Frequency (Hz)	50	63	80	100	125	160	200	250	315	400	500	630
Normalized Level (dB)	26.5	39.9	47.5	53.7	60.5	59.6	63.6	68.4	68.7	67.4	69.0	69.3
Frequency (Hz)	800	1000	1250	1600	2000	2500	3150	4000	5000	6300	8000	10000
Normalized Level (dB)	69.4	70.0	70.2	72.1	71.8	68.4	64.6	64.5	58.7	51.4	41.2	35.2

This example illustrated the process for developing a spectrum at 1000 feet. The same process is repeated for all 10 INM NPD distances.

Step 3: Acoustic Summation of One-Third Octave-Band Data (All INM Distances)

The mean-squared pressure associated with the spectral data corrected to 1000 feet above (for all 24 one-third octave bands) is then summed and converted to decibels to produce the values of 81.1 (Step 2a) and 80.6 (Step 2b). This is in turn repeated for all 10 INM NPD distances. The table below shows the final step of the process with the delta dB differences computed. This difference, calculated for each of the ten standard INM NPD distances, represents the atmospheric adjustment (AA_{ADJ}) which is applied to the NPD curves.

Distance	A-Weighted ARP-866A (15°C 70%)	A-Weighted SAE-AIR-1845	Difference dB
200	83.2	83.1	0.1
400	82.6	82.3	0.3
630	82.0	81.6	0.4
1000	81.1	80.6	0.5
2000	79.3	78.5	0.8
4000	76.7	75.7	1.0
6300	74.5	73.4	1.1
10000	72.0	70.7	1.3
16000	68.9	67.3	1.6
25000	65.2	63.3	1.9

The A-Weighted levels calculated above are for a normalized spectral class, assuming 70 dB at the 1000 Hz one-third octave-band. The deltas in this example are then applied across all power settings and all A-weighted NPD curves (SEL and LAMAX).

The atmospheric absorption correction for the C-weighted family of noise metrics is calculated similar to the process outlined above using C-weighting in place of A-weighting. The atmospheric absorption adjustment for tone-corrected perceived noise metrics is based on A-weighted spectral data. This process is considered to be a reasonable approximation for these metrics.

3.5   Acoustic Impedance Adjustment (AI$_{ADJ}$)

Before the interpolated/extrapolated noise level data, $L_{P,d}$, is utilized for computations, an acoustic impedance adjustment, designated by the symbol AI$_{ADJ}$, is applied. Acoustic impedance is defined as the product of the density of air and the speed of sound, and it is a function of temperature, atmospheric pressure, and indirectly altitude.

The noise-levels in the INM NPD database are corrected to reference-day conditions: temperature 77 °F, pressure 29.92 inches of mercury, and altitude mean sea level.[10] The noise levels can be adjusted to airport temperature and pressure by:[3,4,17,18]

$$AI_{ADJ} = 10 \log_{10}[\ \rho c\ /\ 409.81\ ] \qquad (dB)$$
$$\rho c = 416.86\ (\delta\ /\ \theta^{\frac{1}{2}})$$

where

AI$_{ADJ}$	acoustic impedance adjustment to be added to noise level data in the INM NPD data base (dB),
ρc	acoustic impedance at observer altitude and pressure (newton-seconds/m^3),
θ	ratio of absolute temperature at the observer to standard-day absolute temperature at sea level,
δ	ratio of atmospheric pressure at the observer to standard-day pressure at sea level.

See Appendix B for a derivation of the AI$_{ADJ}$ equation.

When the terrain elevation enhancement is invoked, AI$_{ADJ}$ is computed and applied to the NPD data on an observer-by-observer basis, according to the observer altitude, temperature, and pressure. Otherwise, the airport elevation and the observer altitude are equivalent, and a single value of AI$_{ADJ}$ is computed and applied, regardless of the observation point.

When terrain elevation is not invoked, and when airport temperature, pressure, and altitude are equal to 77°F, 29.92 in-Hg, and 0 ft MSL, respectively, then AI$_{ADJ}$ is zero.

3.6   Noise Fraction Adjustment for Exposure Metrics (NF$_{ADJ}$)

The exposure-based noise level data interpolated/extrapolated from the INM NPD data, $L_{P,d}$, represents the noise exposure level associated with a flight path of infinite length. However, the aircraft flight path in INM 6.0 is described by a set of finite-length segments, each contributing varying amounts of exposure to the overall noise metric computed at an observer.

The noise fraction algorithm, used exclusively for computation of the exposure-based metrics (L_{AE}, L_{dn}, L_{den}, L_{Aeq24h}, L_d, L_n, L_{CE}, L_{EPN}, L_{NEF}, and L_{WECPN}), and indirectly for computation of the time-above metrics (TA_{ALA}, TA_{ALC}, TA_{PNT}, $\%TA_{ALA}$, $\%TA_{ALC}$, and $\%TA_{PNT}$), computes the fraction of noise exposure associated with a finite-length flight path segment. This fraction of noise exposure is computed relative to the noise associated with a flight path of infinite length. It is based upon a fourth-power, 90-degree dipole model of sound radiation[16,19,20] and its derivation is presented in Appendix C.

Computation of the noise fraction is necessary because the L_{AE}, L_{CE}, and L_{EPN}-based noise levels in the NPD database are computed assuming that an aircraft proceeds along a straight flight path, parallel to the ground, and of infinite length. To obtain the noise exposure level or time-above at an observer location due to an aircraft proceeding along a finite flight-path segment, the exposure-based noise-level data, interpolated/extrapolated from the INM NPD data, must be adjusted by a fractional component, which is associated with the geometry of the observer/flight-segment pair.

3.6.1   Noise Fraction Adjustment for Flight Segments

For an arbitrary segment, the fourth-power time-history model computes noise exposure fraction, F_{12}, as follows:

$$F_{12} = (1/\pi) \left[\alpha_2/(1+\alpha_2^2) + \tan^{-1}\alpha_2 - \alpha_1/(1+\alpha_1^2) - \tan^{-1}\alpha_1 \right]$$

where

$$\alpha_1 = -q_1 / s_L$$
$$\alpha_2 = (-q_1 + L) / s_L$$
$$s_L = s_0 10^{[L_{E.P,d} - L_{Smx.P,d}]/10}$$

and where

q_1 relative distance (feet) from segment start point to point $\mathbf{P_S}$,

L   length of segment (feet),

s_0 171.92 feet for L_{AE} and L_{CE}, or 1719.2 feet for L_{EPN},

$L_{E.P,d}$ unadjusted interpolated NPD noise exposure level (dB) at 160 knots (L_{AE}, L_{CE}, L_{EPN}),

$L_{Smx.P,d}$ unadjusted interpolated NPD maximum noise level (dB) (L_{ASmx}, L_{CSmx}, L_{PNTSmx}).

Both $L_{E.P,d}$ and $L_{Smx.P,d}$ are interpolated from NPD data at a given engine power setting and at a distance SLR_{pth}, which is the distance from the observer to the perpendicular closest point of approach (PCPA) on the extended segment.

The noise fraction is then converted to a dB adjustment:

$$NF_{ADJ} = 10 \log_{10}[F_{12}] \qquad\qquad (dB).$$

3.6.2 Noise Fraction Adjustment for Behind Start-of-Takeoff Roll

For an observer behind the start-of-takeoff ground roll, a special case of the noise fraction equation applies. This special case noise fraction, denoted by the symbol F_{12}', ensures consistency of computed exposure levels that are on a line at azimuth angle of 90° measured from the nose of the aircraft at start of takeoff roll.

$$F_{12}' = (1/\pi) \left[\alpha_2/(1+\alpha_2^2) + \tan^{-1}\alpha_2 \right] 10^{DIR_{ADJ}/10}$$

$$\alpha_2 = L / s_L$$

where L and s_L are defined in the above section and DIR_{ADJ} is the ground based directivity adjustment (see Section 3.9).

The noise fraction for the special case of observers behind the start-of-takeoff roll is then converted to a dB adjustment:

$$NF_{ADJ} = 10 \log_{10}[F_{12}'] \qquad \text{(dB)}.$$

A similar equation is used for observers in front of the end point of the last approach segment.

3.7 Duration Adjustment for Exposure-Based Metrics (DUR$_{ADJ}$)

For exposure-based metrics, consistent with SAE AIR 1845, NPDs are derived for a reference speed of 160 knots. For aircraft speeds other than 160 knots, the duration adjustment is applied to account for the effect of time-varying aircraft speed, both acceleration and deceleration. It is not applied to maximum noise level metrics since they are mostly independent of speed. In addition, since runup operations are stationary operations and they do not have associated speeds, the duration adjustment is not applied.

The L_{AE} and L_{EPN} values in the NPD database are referenced to an aircraft speed of 160 knots. For other aircraft speeds, the aircraft speed adjustment, DUR_{ADJ}, is given by:

$$DUR_{ADJ} = 10 \log_{10}[160 / AS_{seg}] \qquad \text{(dB)}$$

where AS_{seg} is the aircraft speed at the closest point of approach (CPA) for the segment, as discussed in Section 3.2.2.

3.8 Lateral Attenuation Adjustment (LA$_{ADJ}$)

The lateral attenuation adjustment takes into account the following effects on aircraft sound due to over-ground propagation:* (1) ground reflection effects; (2) refraction effects; and (3) airplane shielding effects, as well as other ground and engine/aircraft installation effects. It is computed as a function of two empirical parameters, the sideline distance from the flight-path segment to

---

* The lateral attenuation adjustment in INM was derived from field measurements made over grass-covered, acoustically soft terrain. Consequently, when source-to-receiver propagation occurs primarily over an acoustically hard surface (e.g., water), and the hard surface dominates the study environment, it is possible that INM could under predict the actual noise level.

the observer, l_{seg}, given in Section 3.2.2, and the elevation angle, β, formed by SLR_{seg} and the horizontal plane of the observer location (see Figure 3-5). The ground beneath the observer is defined by a flat plane, regardless of whether the terrain enhancement is invoked or not.

The specific algorithms used for computing lateral attenuation in INM 6.0 depend on whether the model type associated with a particular aircraft is type INM or type NOISEMAP.†

3.8.1 INM Aircraft

If the model type associated with a particular aircraft in the NPD database is categorized as "INM", computation of the lateral attenuation adjustment depends upon whether the aircraft is located on the ground or in the air. If the aircraft is on the ground, the adjustment has a ground-to-ground component only. If the aircraft is in the air, it has both a ground-to-ground and an air-to-ground component. In the latter case, the two components are computed separately and then combined.[21]

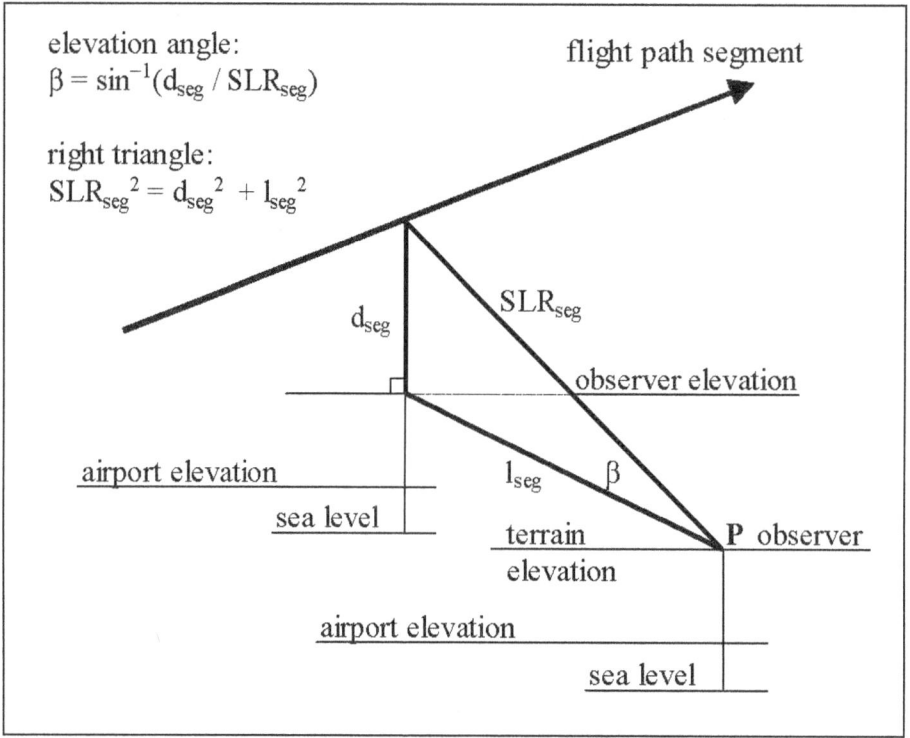

Figure 3-5 Lateral Attenuation Geometry

---

† The INM 6.0 database includes all of the aircraft from the United States Air Force NOISEMAP suite of programs, as of March 2001. The specific NOISEMAP aircraft are identified in the MODEL_TYPE field of the INM 6.0 *NOIS_GRP.DBF* database file, with an "N" for NOISEMAP, as compared to an "I" for INM.

The ground-to-ground component of the lateral attenuation adjustment is computed as follows:

$$G(l_{seg}) = \begin{cases} 15.09 \left[\, 1 - e^{-0.00274\, l_{seg}} \,\right] & \text{for } 0 < l_{seg} \leq 914 \text{ m (3000 ft)} \quad \text{(dB)} \\ \\ 13.86 & \text{for } l_{seg} > 914 \text{ m (3000 ft)} \quad \text{(dB)} \end{cases}$$

where

l_{seg} sideline distance (meters) in the horizontal plane from the observer to the projection of CPA.

The air-to-ground component of the lateral attenuation adjustment, $\Lambda(\beta)$, is computed as follows:

$$\Lambda(\beta) = \begin{cases} 3.96 - 0.066\, \beta + 9.9\, e^{-0.13\, \beta} & \text{for } 0 \leq \beta \leq 60° \quad \text{(dB)} \\ \\ 0 & \text{for } 60 < \beta \leq 90° \quad \text{(dB)} \end{cases}$$

where

β elevation angle (degrees); if $\beta < 0$, β is reset to $0°$.

The overall lateral attenuation adjustment, LA_{ADJ}, which takes into account both the ground-to-ground component, $G(l_{seg})$, and the air-to-ground component, $\Lambda(\beta)$, is then computed as follows:

$$LA_{ADJ\,(INM)} = G(l_{seg})\, \Lambda(\beta)\, /\, 13.86 \qquad \text{(dB)}$$

3.8.2 NOISEMAP Aircraft

If the model type in the NPD database is categorized as "NOISEMAP", computation of the lateral attenuation adjustment depends upon the elevation angle, β. If the elevation angle is less then 2 degrees, the adjustment has a ground-to-ground component only. If the elevation angle is greater than or equal to 2 degrees, it has both a ground-to-ground and an air-to-ground component. In the latter case, the two components are computed separately and then combined.

The ground-to-ground component of the lateral attenuation adjustment is computed as follows:*

$$G(l_{seg}) = \begin{cases} 15.09 \left[\, 1 - e^{-0.00274\, l_{seg}} \,\right] & \text{for } 0 < l_{seg} \leq 401 \text{ m (1316 ft)} \quad \text{(dB)} \\ \\ 10.06 & \text{for } l_{seg} > 401 \text{ m (1316 ft)} \quad \text{(dB)} \end{cases}$$

where

l_{seg} sideline distance (meters) in the horizontal plane from the observer to the projection of CPA.

The air-to-ground component of the lateral attenuation adjustment is computed as follows:

$$\Lambda(\beta) = \begin{cases} (\, 21.056\, /\, \beta\,) - 0.468 & \text{for } 2 \leq \beta \leq 45° \quad \text{(dB)} \\ \\ 0 & \text{for } 45 < \beta \leq 90° \quad \text{(dB)} \end{cases}$$

where

β elevation angle (degrees); if $\beta < 0$, β is reset to $0°$.

---

* The ground-to-ground component of the lateral attenuation adjustment actually computed by the NOISEMAP program depends on the one-third octave-band frequency characteristics of the noise source. Due to this fact, small differences are expected when comparing INM and NOISEMAP results directly, especially in the immediate vicinity of the airport runways.

The overall lateral attenuation adjustment, LA_{ADJ}, which takes into account both the ground-to-ground component, $G(l_{seg})$, and the air-to-ground component, $\Lambda(\beta)$, for $2° \leq \beta$, is then computed as follows:

$$LA_{ADJ\,(NOISEMAP)} = G(l_{seg})\,\Lambda(\beta)\,/\,10.06 \qquad\qquad \text{(dB)}.$$

3.9 Ground-Based Directivity Adjustment (DIR_{ADJ})

For the special case of computing noise behind the start-of-takeoff ground roll, as well as for computing metrics associated with runup operations, a field-measurement-based directivity adjustment is employed. This directivity adjustment is expressed as a function of azimuth angle, θ, defined as the angle formed by the direction of the nose of the aircraft and the line connecting the aircraft to the observer.[16]

To account for the effect of slight variations in the heading of the aircraft just prior to takeoff ground roll, among other effects, a directivity smoothing adjustment, computed as a function of slant range from the observer location to the aircraft, is also applied.

The azimuth angle, θ, used in computing the directivity adjustment is given by:

$$\theta = \cos^{-1}(q\,/\,r_1) \qquad \text{(degrees)}$$

where

    q relative distance between points $\mathbf{P}_1$, and $\mathbf{P}_S$ (feet). By definition, the value of q is negative (see Figures 3.2 – 3.4);

    r_1 SLR_{seg}, the slant range from the observer to the start of takeoff roll (feet).

Since the value of q is negative, and the value of SLR_{seg} is positive, the value of θ is greater than 90° when the observer is behind start of takeoff.

The directivity adjustment, DIR_{ADJ} is computed as a function of azimuth angle.
For θ between 90° and 148.4°,

$$DIR_{ADJ} = 51.44 - 1.553\,\theta + 0.015147\,\theta^2 - 0.000047173\,\theta^3 \qquad \text{(dB)}.$$

For θ between 148.4° and 180°,

$$DIR_{ADJ} = 339.18 - 2.5802\,\theta - 0.0045545\,\theta^2 + 0.000044193\,\theta^3 \qquad \text{(dB)}.$$

The directivity adjustment, DIR_{ADJ}, is modified by a smoothing equation that is computed as a function of slant range from the observer location to start of takeoff, SLR_{seg}. The smoothing function is activated when SLR_{seg} is greater than 2500 feet. The function, which reduces the directivity by a factor of 50 percent per doubling of distance, is given by:

$$DIR_{ADJ} = DIR_{ADJ}\,(2500\,/\,SLR_{seg}) \qquad \text{(dB)}$$

for $SLR_{seg} > 2500$ feet.

3.10 Computation of Exposure-Based Noise Level Metrics

This section discusses the computation of exposure-based noise level metrics for flight operations (Section 3.10.2), as well as for runup operations (Section 3.10.3). To obtain the total noise exposure at an observer location, the contributions from both flight operations and runup operations are combined.

For the computation of exposure-based metrics at multiple observers in a regular grid, including the base regular grid used in a single-metric and multi-metric contour analysis, the methodology described in Sections 3.2 through 3.10 is repeated iteratively. If the terrain elevation enhancement is not invoked, the step of computing the acoustic impedance adjustment (Section 3.5) for each observer iteration is skipped. It is not necessary to repeat this step if the terrain elevation enhancement is inactive because the observer's elevation, temperature, and pressure are the same as at the airport.

3.10.1 System Adjustments

Prior to the calculation of noise metrics for flight and runup operations, described in the following Sections 3.10.2 and 3.10.3, INM applies study-wide adjustments to the interpolated NPD data. These include an atmospheric absorption adjustment (AA_{ADJ}, Section 3.4) and an acoustic impedance adjustment (AI_{ADJ}, Section 3.5). In the case when terrain elevation processing is utilized, only the atmospheric absorption adjustment is applied study-wide.

a) Study-wide atmospheric absorption (AA_{ADJ}) and acoustic impedance (AI_{ADJ}) adjustments

Prior to application of the segment adjustments highlighted in Sections 3.6 through 3.9, study-wide atmospheric absorption and acoustic impedance adjustments are applied to the NPD values that are used for noise level interpolation (Section 3.3). In effect, noise level interpolation is undertaken utilizing adjusted NPD curves per the following:

$$L_{E,p,d\text{-}ADJ} = L_{E,P,d} + [AA_{ADJ} + AI_{ADJ}]_{study\text{-}wide}$$
$$L_{Smx,P,d\text{-}ADJ} = L_{Smx,P,d} + [AA_{ADJ} + AI_{ADJ}]_{study\text{-}wide}$$

b) Study-wide atmospheric absorption adjustment (AA_{ADJ}) and observer-based acoustic impedance adjustment (AI_{ADJ})

For studies that utilize terrain elevation processing, the acoustic impedance adjustment is applied separately for each observer, using the terrain elevation at the observer's location instead of the airport elevation. For studies with terrain elevation processing, noise level interpolation is undertaken by first adjusting NPD curves using study-wide atmospheric absorption, and then the acoustic impedance adjustment is added to the sound levels after noise level interpolation:

$$L_{E,p,d\text{-}ADJ} = L_{E,P,d} + [AA_{ADJ}]_{study\text{-}wide} + [AI_{ADJ}]_{per\text{-}observer}$$
$$L_{Smx,P,d\text{-}ADJ} = L_{Smx,P,d} + [AA_{ADJ}]_{study\text{-}wide} + [AI_{ADJ}]_{per\text{-}observer}$$

3.10.2 Flight Operations

For the exposure-based noise metrics, the sound exposure ratio due to a single flight-path segment of a flight operation, denoted by the symbol E_{seg}, is computed as follows:

$$E_{seg} = 10^{[L_{E.P,d\text{-}ADJ} + NF_{ADJ} + DUR_{ADJ} - LA_{ADJ} + DIR_{ADJ}] / 10}$$

where

$L_{E.P,d\text{-}ADJ}$ L_{AE}, L_{CE}, or L_{EPN}, in dB, resulting from the noise interpolation process using NPD data (Section 3.3) and atmospheric absorption and acoustic impedance adjustments (Section 3.10.1);

NF_{ADJ} noise fraction adjustment, in dB (see Section 3.6);

DUR_{ADJ} aircraft speed duration adjustment, in dB (see Section 3.7);

LA_{ADJ} lateral attenuation adjustment, in dB (see Section 3.8);

DIR_{ADJ} directivity adjustment, in dB, which is applied only if the flight-path segment is part of takeoff ground roll (see Section 3.9).

Each flight in the study case has associated with it a given number of operations for the day, evening, and night-time periods. Also, depending upon the user-specified metric, each time period may have a weighting factor, i.e., a noise penalty, associated with it. The weighting factors for the standard exposure-based metrics, along with their associated time-averaging constants N_T, which are discussed later in this section, are summarized in Table 3-2.

INM 6.0 users also have the option to define their own weighting factors and averaging constants through the use of a user-specified exposure-based metric.

The number of operations associated with each time period, coupled with the weighting factors, is used to compute the weighted sound exposure ratio, denoted by the symbol $E_{wt.seg}$, for a single flight-path segment and operation.

$$E_{wt.seg} = [W_{day} N_{day} + W_{eve} N_{eve} + W_{ngt} N_{ngt}] E_{seg}$$

where

N_{day} number of user-specified operations between 0700 and 1900 hours local time;

N_{eve} number of user-specified operations between 1900 and 2200 hours local time;

N_{ngt} number of user-specified operations between 2200 and 0700 hours local time;

W_{day} day-time weighting factor, either standard or user-defined (see Table 3-2 for the standard weighting factors associated with a particular exposure-based noise level metric);

W_{eve} evening weighting factor, either standard or user-defined;

W_{ngt} night-time weighting factor, either standard or user-defined;

E_{seg} sound exposure ratio at an observer location due to a single flight-path segment of a flight operation.

Table 3-2 Weighting Factors and Time-Averaging Constants
for the Standard Exposure-Based Metrics

Metric	W_{day}	W_{eve}	W_{ngt}	N_T	$10 \log_{10}[N_T]$ (dB)
L_{AE}	1	1	1	1	0
L_{dn}	1	1	10	86400	49.37
L_{den}	1	$3^{\#}$	10	86400	49.37
L_{Aeq24h}	1	1	1	86400	49.37
L_d	1	1	0	54000	47.32
L_n	0	0	1	32400	45.11
L_{CE}	1	1	1	1	0
L_{EPN}	1	1	1	1	0
L_{NEF}	1	1	16.67	630957345	88.0*
L_{WECPN}	1	$3^{\#}$	10	8640†	39.37

The weighted sound exposure ratio for each segment, $E_{wt.seg(i)}$, is computed iteratively and preserved.

The weighted sound exposure ratio due to an entire flight operation is obtained by summing the ratios associated with each segment in the flight path. The weighted sound exposure ratio for a flight operation, $E_{wt.flt}$, is computed as follows:

$$E_{wt.flt} = \sum_{i=1}^{n_{seg}} E_{wt.seg(i)}$$

where n_{seg} is the number of segments in the three-dimensional flight path.

\# In accordance with the technical definition, a 5 dB penalty is added to evening operations when computing the L_{den} noise metric. The 5 dB penalty, expressed in terms of a weighting factor, is equivalent to 3.16, not 3. However, in Title 21, Subchapter 6, §5001 of California state law a factor of 3 is used. Since the state of California is the primary user of the L_{den} metric, it was decided that INM would be consistent with state law, rather than the traditional technical definition. The evening weighting factor in the L_{WECPN} metric was changed to 3 for consistency. It is anticipated that this small difference will be of no practical consequence in the computations.

* The 88.0 dB value is an arbitrarily chosen scaling constant inherent in the definition of the L_{NEF} metric. A 24-hour period is used to compute the metric.

† The 8640 value is the number of 10-second intervals in a 24-hour period. Unlike L_{AE} and L_{CE}, which are normalized to a duration of $t_o = 1$ second, L_{EPN} is normalized to a duration of $t_o = 10$ seconds.

The weighted sound exposure ratio for all flight operations in the entire study case is obtained by summing the ratios associated with each flight operation. The weighted sound exposure ratio for all flight operations in the study case, $E_{wt.arpt}$, is computed as follows:

$$E_{wt.arpt} = \sum_{k=1}^{n_{flt}} E_{wt.flt(k)}$$

where n_{flt} is the number of flight operations in the study case.

The mean-square sound-pressure ratio associated with a specific exposure-based noise level metric is computed by dividing the weighted sound exposure ratio for the related base metric, $E_{wt.aprt}$, by a time-averaging constant N_T, either standard or user-specified. The time-averaging constants for the standard exposure-based metrics were summarized in Table 3-2. Note that three of the exposure-base metrics (L_{AE}, L_{CE}, and L_{EPN}) are true sound exposure levels, and they are not divided by a time-averaging constant (or, equivalently, they are divided by 1).

The average or equivalent mean-square sound-pressure ratio, P, associated with an exposure-based metric, is given by:

$$P_{wt.arpt} = E_{wt.arpt} / N_T .$$

The final step in the process is to convert $P_{wt.arpt}$ to its equivalent dB value. The dB value for a user-specified, exposure-based metric due to all flight operations in an airport case is computed as follows:

$$L_{E.wt.arpt} = 10 \log_{10}[P_{wt.arpt}] \qquad (dB)$$

$L_{E.wt.arpt}$ is a standard exposure-based noise level metric or a user-specified exposure-based metric, depending upon the specific weighting factors and time-averaging constants selected.

In addition to the above calculations, the single-event, <u>unweighted</u> sound exposure level, $L_{E.flt}$, for each flight operation is computed iteratively and saved for use in the time-above calculation (see Section 3.12.1).

$$L_{E.flt} = 10 \log_{10}[\sum_{i=1}^{n_{seg}} E_{seg(i)}] \qquad (dB)$$

3.10.3 Runup Operations

For the exposure-based noise metrics, the mean-square sound-pressure ratio due to a single runup operation, denoted by the symbol P_{runup}, is computed as follows:

$$P_{runup} = 10^{[L_{Smx.,P,d-ADJ} - LA_{ADJ} + DIR_{ADJ}]/10}$$

where

$L_{Smx.,P,d-ADJ}$ L_{ASmx}, L_{CSmx}, or L_{PNTSmx}, in dB, resulting from noise interpolation (Sections 3.3) and adjustment process (Section 3.10.1),

DIR_{ADJ} directivity adjustment, in dB (Section 3.9),

and all other variables are defined in Section 3.10.2.

As is the case with flight operations, each runup in the study case has associated with it a given number of operations for the day, evening, and night-time periods. Also, depending upon the user-specified metric, each time period may have a weighting factor associated with it. The main difference in computing an exposure-based metric for a flight operation as compared with a runup operation, is that the runup also has associated with it a time duration.

The number of operations associated with each time period, coupled with the weighting factors and the runup duration, are used to compute the weighted sound exposure ratio, $E_{wt.runup}$, for a single runup operation:

$$E_{wt.runup} = [W_{day} N_{day} + W_{eve} N_{eve} + W_{ngt} N_{ngt}] (t_{runup}/t_o) P_{runup}$$

where

t_{runup} runup duration (seconds);

t_o 1 second for L_{ASmx}, or 10 seconds for L_{PNTSmx};

and all other variables are defined in Section 3.10.2.

All subsequent steps required for computing exposure-based noise levels for runup operations are identical to those described in Section 3.10.2 for a flight operation. Specifically, the weighted sound exposure ratio for each runup operation is computed iteratively and preserved. Each ratio is then arithmetically summed for all runup operations in the airport case, a time averaging constant is applied and the ratio is converted to a decibel value.

3.11 Computation of Maximum Noise Level Metrics

This section discusses separately the computation of maximum noise level metrics for flight operations (Section 3.11.1), as well as for runup operations (Section 3.11.2). To obtain the maximum noise level at an observer location, the contributions from both flight operations and runup operations are considered.

For the computation of maximum noise level metrics at multiple observers in a regular grid, including the base regular grid used in a single-metric and multi-metric contour analysis, the methodology described in Sections 3.2 through 3.9, as well as that described in Section 3.10, is repeated iteratively. If the terrain elevation enhancement is not invoked, the step of computing the acoustic impedance adjustment (Section 3.5) for each observer location is skipped. It is not necessary to repeat this step if the terrain elevation enhancement is inactive because the observer's elevation, temperature, and pressure are the same as at the airport.

3.11.1 Flight Operations

The maximum noise level due to a single flight-path segment, $L_{Smx.seg}$, is computed as follows:

$$L_{Smx.seg} = L_{Smx.P,d} + AA_{ADJ} + AI_{ADJ} - LA_{ADJ} + DIR_{ADJ} \quad (dB)$$

where

$L_{Smx.P,d}$ unadjusted, L_{ASmx}, L_{CSmx}, or L_{PNTSmx}, in dB, resulting from the noise interpolation process (Section 3.3),

AA_{ADJ} atmospheric absorption adjustment, in dB (Section 3.4),

AI_{ADJ} acoustic impedance adjustment, in dB (Section 3.5),

LA$_{ADJ}$ lateral attenuation adjustment, in dB (Section 3.8),

DIR$_{ADJ}$ directivity adjustment, in dB, which is applied only if the flight-path segment is part of takeoff ground roll (Section 3.9).

The maximum noise level associated with each flight-path segment in a flight operation, L$_{Smx.seg(i)}$, is computed iteratively and preserved.

The maximum noise level associated with each flight operation, L$_{Smx.flt}$, is then determined by performing a flight-segment by flight-segment comparison of L$_{Smx.seg}$ values, and preserving the largest value associated with each flight. L$_{Smx.flt}$ is computed as follows:

$$L_{Smx.flt} = \overset{n_{seg}}{\underset{i=1}{\text{Max}}}[\, L_{Smx.seg(i)} \,]$$

where n$_{seg}$ is the number of segments in the three-dimensional flight path.

The maximum noise level associated with each flight operation in the airport case, L$_{Smx.flt(k)}$, is computed iteratively and saved.

The L$_{Smx.flt(k)}$ values are grouped according to the time period within which they occur, day, evening, or night.

The maximum noise level associated with each time period, t, is computed as follows:

$$L_{Smx(t)} = \overset{n_{flt(t)}}{\underset{k=1}{\text{Max}}}[\, L_{Smx.flt(k)} \,]$$

where n$_{flt(t)}$ is the number of flight operations in the study case for a given time period, t.

Given three L$_{Smx(t)}$ values, one for each time period, day, evening and night, the user is given the option to select a time period, either day, evening, or night, or any combination thereof, for which the maximum noise level is to be determined.

$$L_{Smx} = \text{Max}[\, L_{Smx(day)}W_{day}, \, L_{Smx(eve)}W_{eve}, \, L_{Smx(ngt)}W_{ngt}) \,]$$

where

Max[ ]	function that returns the maximum of three noise level values,
L$_{Smx(day)}$	maximum noise level for the time period between 0700 and 1900 hours local time,
L$_{Smx(eve)}$	maximum noise level for the time period between 1900 and 2200 hours local time,
L$_{Smx(ngt)}$	noise level for the time period between 2200 and 0700 hours local time,
W$_{day}$	day-time weighting factor, either zero or one, depending on whether that time period should be considered by the Max function,
W$_{eve}$	evening weighting factor, either zero or one,
W$_{ngt}$	night-time weighting factor, either zero or one.

L$_{Smx}$ is equivalent to either the maximum A-weighted sound level, with slow-scale exponential weighting characteristics (L$_{ASmx}$), the maximum C-weighted sound level, with slow-scale exponential weighting characteristics (L_{CSmx}), or the tone-corrected maximum perceived noise level, with slow-scale exponential weighting characteristics (L_{PNTSmx}). L_{Smx} is expressed in dB.

3.11.2 Runup Operations

The maximum noise level due to a single runup operation, denoted by the symbol $L_{Smx.runup}$, is computed as follows:

$$L_{Smx.runup} = L_{Smx.P,d} + AA_{ADJ} + AI_{ADJ} - LA_{ADJ} + DIR_{ADJ} \qquad \text{(dB)}$$

where DIR_{ADJ} is the directivity adjustment, in dB (Section 3.9); and all other variables are defined in Section 3.11.1.

As is the case with flight operations, the maximum noise level associated with each runup operation is computed iteratively and preserved.

All subsequent steps required for computing maximum noise levels for runup operations are the same as those described in Section 3.11.1 for a flight operation. Specifically, the $L_{Smx.runup}$ values are grouped according to the time period within which they occur, the maximum value for each time period is determined, and the specific time period or combination of periods is selected for determining the maximum level associated with runup operations.

3.12 Computation of Time-Above Metrics

This section discusses separately the computation of the time above or percent time-above a noise level threshold for flight operations (Section 3.12.1), as well as for runup operations (Section 3.12.2). To obtain the time above or percent time-above at an observer location, the contribution from both flight operations and runup operations are combined.

For the computation of time-above or percent time-above at multiple observers in a regular grid, including the base regular grid used in a single-metric and multi-metric contour analysis, the methodology described in Sections 3.2 through 3.9, as well as that described in Section 3.10, is repeated iteratively. When computing time-above or percent time-above at multiple grid points the user is given the option to define the threshold level for each unique point. For contour computations, a user has the ability to specify a file of threshold or ambient values which can be used for time above or percent time above computations. If the terrain elevation enhancement is not invoked, the step of computing the acoustic impedance adjustment (Section 3.5) for each observer iteration is skipped. It is not necessary to repeat this step if the terrain elevation enhancement is inactive because the observer's elevation, temperature, and pressure are the same as at the airport.

An important assumption inherent in time-above and percent time-above computations is that operations do not overlap in time, i.e., user-specified operations occur in a serial fashion. However, if an airport has parallel runways with operations occurring simultaneously, this assumption is invalid and the computed time-above or percent time-above metric may be larger than what would be measured at the airport. In such instances, a user could define operations in terms of equivalent numbers of serial operations, as compared with average-annual day operations.

3.12.1 Flight Operations

The time-above metric due to a single flight operation is computed by the equation:

$$TA_{flt} = (4/\pi)\, t_o\, 10^{[L_{E.flt} - L_{Smx.flt}]/10}\, [10^{[L_{Smx.flt} - L_0]/20} - 1]^{\frac{1}{2}} / 60 \qquad (minutes)$$

where

t_o 1 second for L_{AE} and L_{cE}, or 10 seconds for L_{EPN},

$L_{E.flt}$ adjusted noise exposure level for the flight (dB), L_{AE}, L_{CE}, L_{EPN} (Section 3.10.2),

$L_{Smx.flt}$ adjusted maximum noise level for the flight (dB), L_{ASmx}, L_{CSmx}, L_{PNTSmx} ($L_{Smx.flt}$ must be larger than L_0),

L_0 user-specified noise-level threshold (dB), expressed as A-weighted noise level, C-weighted noise level, or tone-corrected perceived noise level.

See Appendix C for a derivation of the time-above equation.

Each flight in the study case has associated with it a set number of operations for the day, evening, and night-time periods, along with weighting factors. In the case of the TA metric, the weighting factors act as binary switches, allowing the user to select/deselect specific time periods over which to compute TA. The number of operations associated with each time period, coupled with the weighting factors, are used to compute the weighted time-above value associated with a specific flight operation:

$$TA_{wt.flt} = [\, W_{day}\, N_{day} + W_{eve}\, N_{eve} + W_{ngt}\, N_{ngt}\,]\, TA_{flt} \qquad (minutes)$$

where

N_{day} number of user-specified operations between 0700 and 1900 hours local time,

N_{eve} number of user-specified operations between 1900 and 2200 hours local time,

N_{ngt} number of user-specified operations between 2200 and 0700 hours local time,

W_{day} day-time weighting factor, either zero or one, depending on whether that time period should be considered;

W_{eve} evening weighting factor, either zero or one;

W_{ngt} night-time weighting factor, either zero or one.

The weighted TA for each flight operation in the study case is computed iteratively and preserved.

The time-above metric for all flight operations in the entire study case is then obtained by summing the $TA_{wt.flt}$ values associated with each operation. The time above for all flight operations in the study case, $TA_{wt.aprt}$, is computed as follows:

$$TA_{wt.aprt} = \sum_{k=1}^{n_{flt}} TA_{wt.flt(k)} \qquad (minutes)$$

where n_{flt} is the number of flight operations in the airport case.

TA is equivalent to either the time above an A-weighted sound level (TA_{LA}), the time-above a C-weighted sound level (TA_{LC}), or the time above a tone-corrected perceived noise level (TA_{LPNT}), depending on the metric family selected, either the A-weighted, C-weighted, or the tone-corrected perceived. TA is expressed in minutes.

For percent time-above metrics (%TA_{LA}, %TA_{LC}, and %TA_{LPNT}), the total time in minutes is divided by the user-defined time period of interest (in minutes) and multiplied by 100 percent.

3.12.2 Runup Operations

The time-above metric due to a single runup operation is the portion of the runup time during which the user-specified noise level threshold is exceeded by the runup noise. The time-above for a runup operation is computed as follows:

$$TA_{runup} = \begin{cases} T_{runup} & \text{when } L_{Smx} > L_0 \\ 0 & \text{when } L_{Smx} \leq L_0 \end{cases}$$

where T_{runup} is the time-above duration (minutes) of the runup event, L_{Smx} is one of three types of adjusted maximum noise levels, and L_0 is the time-above noise threshold level.

All subsequent steps required for computing time above for runup operations are identical to those described in Section 3.12.1 for a flight operation. Specifically, the weighted TA for each runup operation is computed iteratively and preserved. Each TA value is then arithmetically summed for all runup operations in the study case.

In the case of percent TA metrics the summed time is divided by the user-defined time period of interest (in minutes) and multiplied by 100 percent.

3.13   Single-Metric vs. Multi-Metric Computations

The difference between single-metric and multi-metric contour computations is in the way the weighting factors (W_{day}, W_{eve}, W_{ngt}) and the time-averaging constants (N_T) are applied during different steps of the computation process.

3.13.1 Single-Metric

For single-metric contour computations, the weighting factors and time averaging constants are known prior to computations. As such, they are considered in the step-by-step computation processes described in Sections 3.10 through 3.12.

3.13.2   Multi-Metric

For multi-metric contour computations, the weighting factors and time-averaging constants are not known prior to computations, and as such, are not considered in the initial computations described in Sections 3.10 through 3.12. Instead, computations are performed independently within each time period, day, evening and night, and once complete, a user is given the capability to apply the weighting factors and time-averaging constants after the bulk of the computations are done.

The primary advantage of the multi-metric mode is that it gives a user the flexibility to choose several metrics within a particular noise family for computations, either the A-weighted, the C-weighted, or the perceived noise family, without having to re-run the majority of the computations. In other words, once a multi-metric contour computation within the A-weighted family of metrics is completed, a user has the ability to display the noise level contours for any or all of the metrics within the A-weighted family.

However, there are two disadvantages to multi-metric contour computations: (1) the initial set of bulk computations tend to be a bit slower as compared with those for the single-metric computations, primarily because the single-metric computations have an additional time-saving feature which is discussed in detail in Section 4.2, i.e., the low/high contour cutoff test; and (2) there are some inherent differences associated with this method when computing other than exposure-based noise level contours. These differences have to do with the way noise significance testing is done, and they are described in Chapter 4.

4   RECURSIVELY-SUBDIVIDED IRREGULAR GRID DEVELOPMENT

As discussed in Chapter 1, INM 6.0 computes noise-level or time-above metrics in the vicinity of an airport and presents the results in one of two formats: (1) noise-level or time-above values at observer positions; or (2) a plot of contours of user-specified noise levels or time-above values. The basic methodology presented in Chapter 3 describes the computation of noise metrics at a single point or for an evenly-spaced regular grid of points. The development of the recursively-subdivided irregular grid of points requires additional discussion.

When performing a contour analysis, INM 6.0 computes noise-level or time-above values for each observer location in a regular base grid, using the methodology described in Chapter 3. The size of the base grid depends on a user-specified case analysis window. The number of points in the base grid is dynamically scaled up or down to provide a grid point spacing of one nautical mile or less. INM creates a recursively-subdivided irregular grid of observers inside the base grid. The density of points in the irregular grid depends on user-specified contour accuracy. Noise levels or time-above values are calculated at each grid point.

Noise-level or time-above contours are developed from the recursively-subdivided irregular grid noise data using a module derived from the United States Air Force NMPLOT Version 4.6 computer program.[22] NMPLOT constructs a contour by (1) computing the Delaunay Triangulation of the grid points, (2) finding a rough contour by drawing straight contour segments through each triangle in the triangulation, and (3) smoothing the rough contour by using cubic splines under tension.*

NMPLOT is an integral component of the NOISEMAP model that is used to predict noise in the vicinity of airports dominated by military operations.[11] To a certain extent, NMPLOT has become the standard contouring program in the transportation-related noise modeling industry. In addition to INM and NOISEMAP, NMPLOT is also used to compute sound level contours for the Federal Highway Administration's Traffic Noise Model (FHWA TNM®), which is used for predicting noise in the vicinity of highways and for designing highway noise barriers.[23]

4.1   Determination of Noise/Time Significant Flight Segments

After computing the regular base grid, the first step in the process of developing the recursively-subdivided grid is to determine which flight segments in a study case are noise- or time-significant at each observer location in the base grid. The purpose of determining significant flight segments is to help reduce the run-time associated with an INM contour computation.

In versions previous to INM 6.0, noise/time significance was performed on a per flight path basis. If an INM study case had 1000 flight paths, there might be 50,000 flight path segments. Rather than evaluating 1000 flight paths for noise significant contributions, INM 6.0 evaluates

---

* The NMPlot Version 4.6 User's Guide is available from Wasmer Consulting at http://www.wasmerconsulting.com.

the 50,000 flight path segments. Even though there are overhead calculations associated with this new segment-based approach, a small increase in calculation precision and a modest decrease in runtime are obtained.

Two separate tests are performed by INM 6.0 to determine if a flight segment is noise significant: (1) a relative noise-level/time test, and (2) a flight segment proximity test. These tests are performed at each observer location making up the base grid. The significance information is then used to guide the process of sub-dividing the base grid to improve contour precision.

4.1.1   Relative Noise-Level/Time Test

In the relative noise-level/time test, all flight segments are sorted, high-to-low, on the basis of their relative noise/time contribution to an observer in the base grid. If a user specifies that a single-metric contour analysis be computed, the sorted list takes into account the weighted segment associated with the specific metric. If a user specifies that a family of metrics (A-weighted, C-weighted, or tone-corrected perceived noise) contour analysis be computed, the sorted list cannot take into account weighted segments, since they are not yet known. Instead, three sorted lists are developed, one for each of the three time periods (day, evening, and night).

The total noise (or time) value at a base-grid observer location is computed by summing the sound exposure ratios (or time-above values) over all flight operations. A running total noise value is also computed from the sorted list of segments, beginning with the flight segment having the largest contribution to the noise, and proceeding through the ordered list. The running noise value is continually compared to the total noise value at a base-grid observer location. When the running value exceeds 97 percent of the total value, the running value is considered complete, and all subsequent flight segments in the sorted list are marked insignificant.

In the case of the exposure-based and time-above metrics, the 97 percent criterion guarantees that the significant-segment noise level is within 0.1 dB and that the time-above is within 3 percent of the total noise/time computed using all the flight segments.

For maximum noise-level metrics, the 97 percent criterion is not used, since the summation of maximum noise-level metrics is not meaningful. In the relative noise-level test for maximum noise-level metrics only one flight segment is considered significant, the one representing the maximum sound level at an observer location.

4.1.2   Segment Proximity Test

In addition to the relative noise-level/time test, a flight segment proximity test is performed on all segments that are marked noise-insignificant. This test uses the diagonal distance between base grid points (approximately 1.4 nautical miles) as an acceptance criterion. If any part of a flight segment is within the diagonal distance of the base grid point being tested, then the flight segment is re-instated as being significant.

4.2   Grid Development

To generate a recursively-subdivided grid, INM first organizes the base grid into grid working areas, each containing nine observer locations (see Figure 4-1). The number of grid working areas depends on the size of the user-defined case analysis window. The base grid is dynamically scaled up or down to provide spacing between base grid points of approximately one nautical mile. For a case analysis window that is 16 x 16 nautical miles, there will be 64 working areas.

4.2.1   Low/High Contour Cutoff Splitting Test

A low/high cutoff contour test is performed on all working areas in the base grid for single-metric contour analyses. Similar to the two noise significance tests, the primary purpose of this test is to speed up the grid-development process.

If all nine noise-level or time-above values within a given working area are sufficiently below/above user-defined minimum/maximum contour levels, further computations are unnecessary, and splitting of the working area is not performed.

4.2.2   Tolerance and Refinement Splitting Tests

A tolerance/refinement splitting test is used to iteratively develop a recursively subdivided irregular grid. The splitting test compares known grid-point values in a nine-point working area to linearly interpolated values. If the interpolated values are within a user-specified tolerance of the known values, or if the user-specified refinement level has been reached, then no splitting is performed.

> The tolerance value is a user-specified value number greater than 0.1 dB or 0.1 minutes. The INM default tolerance value is 1.0 (dB or minutes).

> The refinement level is a user-specified integer between 4 and 18, where 4 represents one level of subdivision of the base grid, and each subsequent refinement level represents an additional level of subdivision. The INM default refinement level is 6, i.e., three levels of subdivision.

For a single-metric contour analysis, the comparison between known values and linearly interpolated values takes into account the weighted operations associated with the specific metric.

For a multi-metric contour analysis, the comparison does not take into account weighted operations because they are not yet known. Instead, three comparisons are performed on three temporary grids, each grid representing the noise/time associated with the day, evening, and night time periods. If the tests performed on any of the three temporary grids warrant a split in a given working area, then the split is performed in a permanent version of the grid. The splitting test for multi-metric contour computations uses a sound exposure metric (L_{AE}, L_{CE}, or L_{EPN}) as the computed test value because the specific metric is not known at the time the grid is being developed. In a multi-metric contour analysis, a user specifies a specific metric after the noise and time values are computed.

Due to the difference between splitting tests, it is possible that a single-metric contour analysis will yield slightly different maximum-level and time-above contours for identical input cases, when compared to a multi-metric analysis. If so, the contours generated by the single-metric analysis may be more accurate.

For the example nine-point working area shown in Figure 4-1 (points A through I), the splitting test proceeds by linearly interpolating values at B, D, E, F, H using the values at A, C, G, I. For example, the interpolated value at B is ½(A + C). Then, eight comparisons are made: calculated B versus interpolated B, calculated E versus interpolated E, etc. There are three horizontal, three vertical, and two diagonal comparisons. If any one of the eight comparisons produces an absolute difference between interpolated and computed values greater than the user-specified tolerance, then the rectangle formed by points A, C, G, and I is subdivided into <u>four</u> new nine-point working areas.

For example, new points (V, W, X, Y, Z) are created in the upper-left quadrant, forming a new nine-point working area. Point V is halfway between points A and B, point W is halfway between points A and D, etc. The noise-levels or time-above values at points V, W, X, Y and Z are then computed using the methodology of Chapter 3, taking into account only noise significant flight operations that are associated with the closest base grid points. For example, since point V is halfway in between points A and B, the noise-significant flights associated with both points are used in the computation.

The above computation iteratively continues until either the user-specified tolerance level or refinement level is achieved.

When the single-metric contour analysis is complete for all base grid working areas, point locations and associated noise-level or time-above values are saved in a pair of binary files, *GRID* and *CONTOUR*. For a multi-metric contour analysis, six binary files (*GRID.MN, GRID.MX, GRID.TA, CONTOUR.MN, CONTOUR.MX, CONTOUR.TA*) are generated; they contain noise exposure, maximum noise level, and time-above data needed to construct a user-specified metric. These various files are further processed to produce the *NMPLOT.GRD* binary file, which the NMPLOT module uses to generate the actual contours.

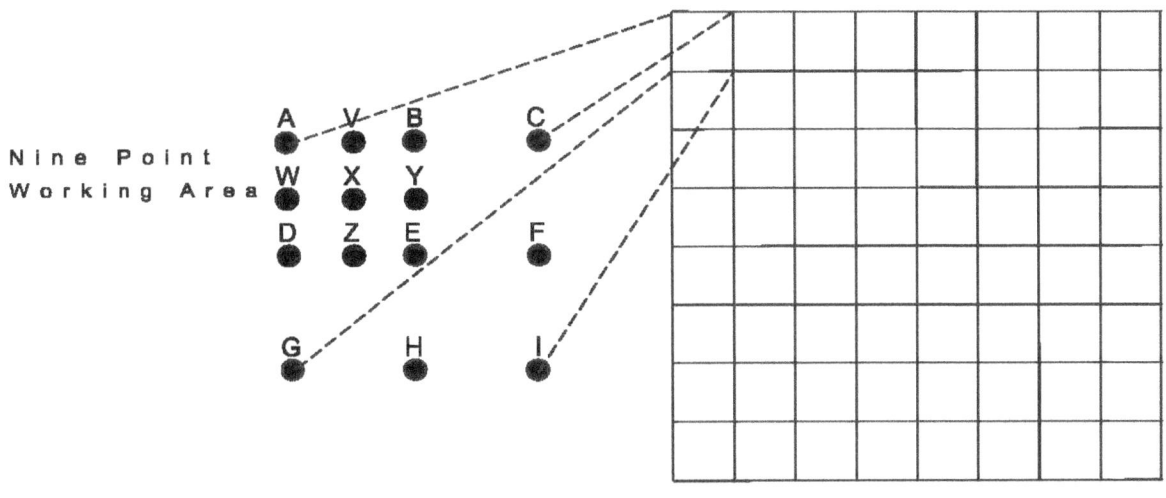

Figure 4-1 Example Grid Area Used for the Generation of Contours

Appendix A: EXAMPLE FLIGHT PATH FILE

The following example file shows data that are passed from the flight path calculation module to the noise calculation module. This is a text version of the INM 6.0 *FLIGHT.PTH* file.

```
INM 6.0
HEADER
   case_id             = D:\INMSTUDY\v60b\test411\CASE1
   aprt_lat            = 39.870431
   aprt_long           = -75.245183
   aprt_elev           = 2500.00
   aprt_temp           = 59.00
   aprt_press          = 29.92
   aprt_humidity       = 70.0
   rs_refine           = 6
   rs_toler            = 1.00
   min_level           = 55.0
   max_level           = 85.0
   run_type            = S
   metric_id           = LAMAX
   fq_type             = A
   metric_type         = M
   metric_weight       = 1.00, 1.00, 1.00
   metric_time         = 0.00
   do_humidity         = 0
   do_terrain          = 0
   ground_type         = S
   terrain_dir         = D:\INMSTUDY\SFO\RWY\Terrain3CD\
   ground_file         =
   ambient_file        =
   do_contour_grid     = 0
   do_standard_grids   = 0
   do_detailed_grids   = 1
   do_100_percent      = 1
   do_metric           = 0, 0, 0, 0, 0, 0, 0, 0, 0, 0, 0, 0, 0
   numb_ngroup         = 12
   numb_noise          = 124
   numb_acft           = 79
   numb_grid           = 1
   numb_pop_pts        = 0
   numb_loc_pts        = 0
```

```
NOISE
0  3JT8DQ A  3000.0 A   96.6  92.8  89.8  86.8  81.8  75.4  71.0  65.6  59.2  52.2
                         96.9  90.2  85.6  80.6  72.8  64.3  58.1  51.2  43.3  34.8
1  3JT8DQ A  6000.0 A  101.8  98.0  95.1  92.0  87.0  80.9  76.2  70.8  64.4  57.4
                        101.1  94.4  89.8  84.8  77.0  68.5  62.3  55.4  47.5  39.0
2  3JT8DQ A  8000.0 D  106.3 102.6  99.7  96.7  91.7  85.7  81.1  75.8  69.6  62.8
                        106.1  99.4  94.8  89.8  82.0  73.6  67.5  60.6  52.9  44.6
3  3JT8DQ A 10000.0 D  111.0 107.2 104.5 101.5  96.6  90.6  86.1  81.0  74.9  68.3
                        111.2 104.5  99.9  95.0  87.2  78.8  72.8  66.1  58.5  50.5
4  3JT8DQ A 12000.0 D  115.8 112.1 109.4 106.5 101.6  95.8  91.3  86.2  80.4  74.1
                        116.6 109.9 105.3 100.4  92.5  84.3  78.4  71.7  64.4  56.6
5  3JT8DQ A 14000.0 D  121.1 117.4 114.8 112.0 107.1 101.4  97.0  92.1  86.4  80.4
                        122.1 115.4 110.8 106.0  98.1  89.9  84.1  77.6  70.4  62.9
6  3JT8DQ P  3000.0 A  100.6  96.4  93.1  89.4  83.4  76.4  71.1  65.0  57.5  48.8
                        108.2 101.2  96.1  90.5  81.7  71.9  64.8  56.8  47.4  36.9
7  3JT8DQ P  6000.0 A  106.4 102.2  98.9  95.2  89.2  82.2  76.9  70.8  63.3  54.6
                        114.0 107.0 101.9  96.3  87.5  77.7  70.6  62.6  53.2  42.7
8  3JT8DQ P  8000.0 D  110.7 106.5 103.3  99.7  93.8  87.1  82.0  76.3  69.3  61.1
                        118.3 111.3 106.3 100.8  92.1  82.6  75.7  68.1  59.2  49.2
9  3JT8DQ P 10000.0 D  115.2 111.2 108.0 104.5  98.8  92.2  87.5  82.1  75.6  68.0
                        122.8 116.0 111.0 105.6  97.1  87.7  81.2  73.9  65.5  56.1
10 3JT8DQ P 12000.0 D  119.4 115.8 112.7 109.3 103.7  97.4  93.0  88.0  82.0  75.0
                        127.0 120.6 115.7 110.4 102.0  92.9  86.7  79.8  71.9  63.1
11 3JT8DQ P 14000.0 D  124.8 120.9 117.9 114.6 109.2 103.1  99.0  94.4  89.0  82.6
                        132.4 125.7 120.9 115.7 107.5  98.6  92.7  86.2  78.9  70.7
(etc.)

AIRCRAFT OPERATIONS
0
  acft_id     = 747200
  eng_type    = J
  owner_cat   = C
  op_type     = R
  numb_ops    = 10.0000, 0.0000, 0.0000
  frst_a_nois = 24
  numb_a_nois = 5
  frst_p_nois = 29
  numb_p_nois = 5
  model_type  = I
  spect_nums  = 207, 107, 0
  runup_id    = A01
  point       = 0.0, 0.0
  heading     = 93.0
  thrust      = 41971.0
  duration    = 1.0
```

```
1
acft_id     = 727Q15
eng_type    = J
owner_cat   = C
op_type     = A
numb_ops    = 19.6000, 0.0000, 2.8000
frst_a_nois = 0
numb_a_nois = 6
frst_p_nois = 6
numb_p_nois = 6
model_type  = I
spect_nums  = 201, 101, 0
flt_path    = A-09R-TR9-0-USER-1
numb_segs   = 20
```

seg	start-x	start-y	start-z	unit-x	unit-y	unit-z	length	speed	d.spd	thrust	d.thr	op
0	-127253.5	-13322.5	6000.0	0.9834	0.1754	-0.0454	6758.2	273.4	-11.8	2495.2	0.0	A
1	-120607.2	-12137.0	5692.9	0.9834	0.1754	-0.0454	6758.2	261.6	-11.8	2495.2	0.0	A
2	-113960.9	-10951.5	5385.8	0.9834	0.1754	-0.0454	6758.2	249.8	-11.8	2495.2	0.0	A
3	-107314.5	-9766.0	5078.7	0.9834	0.1754	-0.0454	6758.2	238.0	-11.8	2495.2	0.0	A
4	-100668.2	-8580.6	4771.6	0.9834	0.1754	-0.0454	6758.2	226.2	-11.8	2495.2	0.0	A
5	-94021.8	-7395.1	4464.4	0.9834	0.1754	-0.0454	6758.2	214.5	-11.8	2495.2	0.0	A
6	-87375.5	-6209.6	4157.3	0.9834	0.1754	-0.0454	6758.2	202.7	-11.8	2495.2	0.0	A
7	-80729.1	-5024.1	3850.2	0.9834	0.1754	-0.0454	6758.2	190.9	-11.8	2495.2	0.0	A
8	-74082.8	-3838.6	3543.1	0.9834	0.1754	-0.0454	6758.2	179.1	-11.8	2495.2	0.0	A
9	-67436.4	-2653.1	3236.0	0.9834	0.1754	-0.0523	8191.4	167.3	-3.9	2495.2	174.6	A
10	-59383.4	-1216.7	2807.3	0.9831	0.1754	-0.0523	8191.4	163.4	-3.9	2669.8	174.6	A
11	-51330.3	219.7	2378.7	0.9899	0.1317	-0.0523	955.7	159.6	-0.4	2844.4	20.4	A
12	-50384.2	345.6	2328.7	0.9986	0.0113	-0.0523	955.7	159.2	-0.4	2864.7	20.4	A
13	-49429.9	356.4	2278.7	0.9981	-0.0329	-0.0523	12128.0	158.7	-5.7	2885.1	258.5	A
14	-37325.1	-42.3	1644.0	0.9981	-0.0329	-0.0523	12169.0	153.0	-3.2	3143.6	1711.0	A
15	-25179.4	-442.4	1007.0	0.9981	-0.0329	-0.0523	12168.9	149.8	-2.2	4854.6	-172.3	A
16	-13033.8	-842.5	370.0	0.9981	-0.0329	-0.0522	7082.3	147.6	-7.6	4682.3	4617.7	A
17	-5965.0	-1075.3	0.0	0.9995	-0.0329	0.0000	1716.8	140.0	-55.0	9300.0	-3875.0	A
18	-4249.2	-1131.9	0.0	0.9995	-0.0329	0.0000	1716.8	85.0	-55.0	5425.0	-3875.0	A
19	-2533.3	-1188.4	0.0	0.9995	-0.0329	0.0000	1.0	30.0	0.0	1550.0	0.0	A

(etc.)

```
GRIDS
0
grid_id    = D01
grid_type  = D
origin     = 11000.2, 2999.8
angle      = 0.0
delta i,j  = 3038.1, 3038.1
numb i,j   = 2, 2
ta_thresh  = 85.0
do_ambient = 0
```

```
delta_amb  = 3.0
do_percent = 0
ref_time   = 24.00
 i  j      X          Y
 0  0   11000.2     2999.8
 0  1   11000.2     6037.8
 1  0   14038.3     2999.8
 1  1   14038.3     6037.8
POPULATION POINTS
LOCATION POINTS
```

Appendix B: ACOUSTIC IMPEDANCE ADJUSTMENT

The majority of noise level data in the INM database were derived from data originally measured during aircraft noise certification tests conducted in accordance with Federal Aviation Regulation, Part 36, "Noise Standards: Aircraft Type and Airworthiness Certification" (FAR Part 36).[10] Section 36.5(c)(1) of FAR Part 36 states that the noise measurements must be corrected to the following [homogeneous] noise certification reference atmospheric conditions:

(i)   Sea level pressure of 2116 psf (76 cm mercury).
(ii)   Ambient temperature of 77 degrees Fahrenheit (25 degrees Celsius).
(iii)   Relative humidity of 70 percent.
(iv)   Zero wind.

The concept of acoustic impedance (denoted by the symbol ρc) is used in INM to correct the reference-day NPD data to the off-reference, non-sea level conditions associated with the user-specified case airport. Acoustic impedance is the product of the density of air and the speed of sound, and it is a function of temperature, atmospheric pressure, and indirectly altitude. An acoustic impedance of 409.81 newton-seconds/m^3 corresponds to the reference atmospheric conditions as defined by FAR Part 36. Acoustic impedance adjustments are made to move from reference-day sea-level conditions to airport-specific temperature and altitude.

Harris[3] and Beranek[4] both contain empirical curves showing acoustic impedance adjustment as a function of temperature and atmospheric pressure (see Figures B-1 and B-2). These curves can be used to obtain a general sense for the magnitude and direction of the adjustment. However they are not appropriate for correcting INM NPD data because the curves are referenced to an acoustic impedance of 406 and 400 newton-seconds/m^3, respectively, not the 409.81 newton-seconds/m^3 associated with NPD reference-day conditions.

The acoustic impedance adjustment is relatively small, usually less than a few tenths of a dB. However, when there is a significant variation in temperature and atmospheric pressure relative to reference-day conditions, the adjustment can be fairly substantial. For example, Denver International Airport is at an elevation of approximately 5000 feet, and assuming a temperature of 70°F and an atmospheric pressure of 29.92 in-Hg, an acoustic impedance adjustment of -0.77 dB is added to NPD noise curves.

The acoustic impedance adjustment is computed by:

$$\text{AI}_{ADJ} = 10 \log_{10}[\, \rho c / 409.81 \,] \qquad (\text{dB})$$

where

$$\rho c = 416.86\,[\, \delta / \theta^{\frac{1}{2}} \,]$$
$$\delta = [(P / 29.92)^{1./5.256} - (0.003566\, A / 518.67)]^{5.256}$$
$$\theta = [459.67 + T - 0.003566\,(A - E)] / 518.67\,.$$

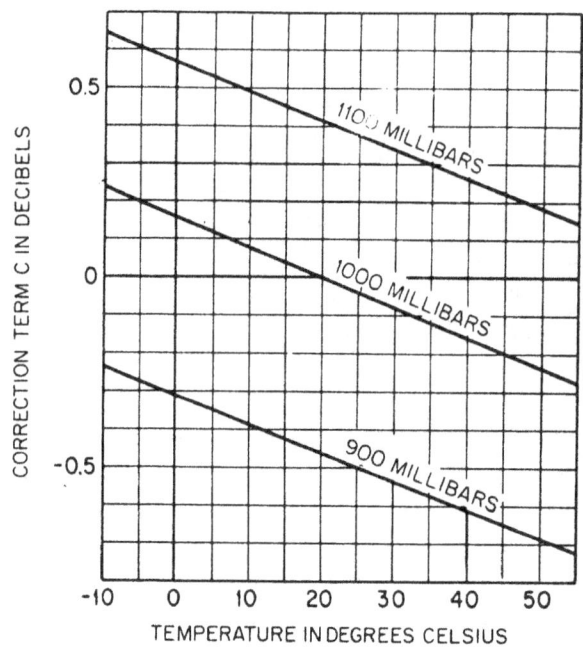

Figure B-1 Acoustic Impedance Adjustment re. 406 newton-second/m³

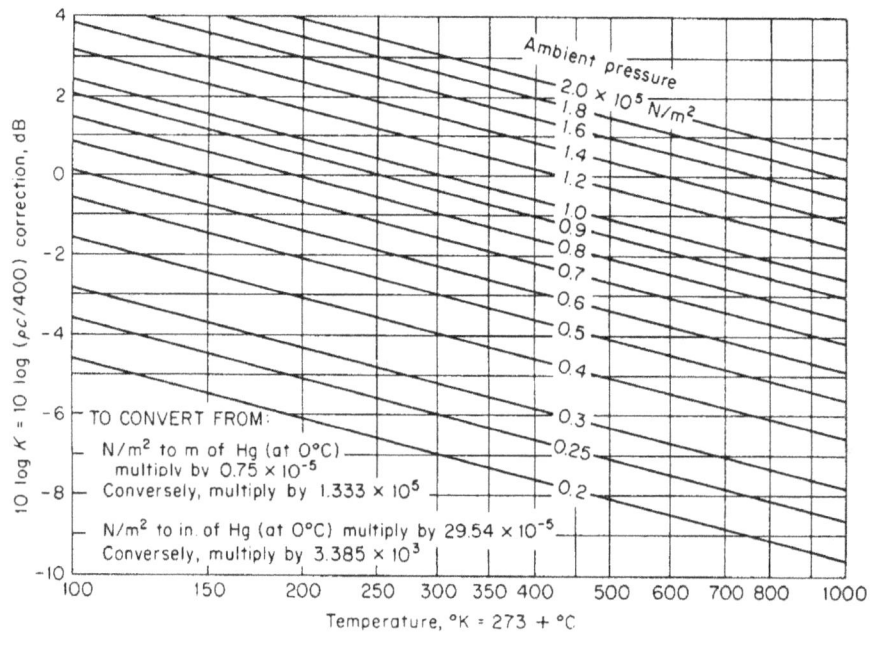

Figure B-2 Acoustic Impedance Adjustment re. 400 newton-second/m³

The variables in the above equations are defined as follows:

AI_{ADJ} acoustic impedance adjustment to be added to noise level data in the INM NPD database (dB),

ρc acoustic impedance at observer altitude and pressure (newton-seconds/m^3),

δ ratio of atmospheric pressure at observer altitude to standard-day pressure at sea level,

θ ratio of absolute temperature at observer altitude to standard-day temperature at sea level,

A   observer elevation MSL (ft),

E   airport elevation MSL (ft),

T   temperature at airport (°F),

P   atmospheric pressure at airport relative to MSL (in-Hg).

The Harris and Beranek references explain the acoustic impedance adjustment in terms of sound intensity and sound pressure. In a free field for plane waves or spherical waves, the sound pressure and particle velocity are in phase, and the magnitude of the intensity (power per unit area) in the direction of propagation of the sound waves is related to the mean-square sound pressure by:

$$I = p^2 / \rho c$$

where

I   sound intensity (power per unit area),

p^2 mean-square sound pressure,

ρc acoustic impedance.

Two sound intensities at a given distance from a given acoustical power source, one measured under actual conditions (no subscript), and the other measured under reference-day conditions ("ref" subscript), are equivalent:

$$p^2 / \rho c = p^2_{ref} / \rho c_{ref} .$$

By rearranging terms and dividing by a constant $p_o = 20$ µPa, the equation becomes:

$$p^2 / p_o^2 = (p^2_{ref} / p_o^2) (\rho c / \rho c_{ref}) .$$

Converting to decibels,

$$10 \log_{10}[p^2 / p_o^2] = 10 \log_{10}[p^2_{ref} / p_o^2] + 10 \log_{10}[\rho c / \rho c_{ref}]$$

and substituting symbols, produces the noise level adjustment equation:

$$L = L_{ref} + 10 \log_{10}[\rho c / \rho c_{ref}] \qquad (dB)$$

where

L corrected NPD level at an airport,

L_{ref} NPD level in the INM database for reference-day conditions,

$10 \log_{10}[\rho c / \rho c_{ref}]$ acoustic impedance adjustment, AI_{ADJ} (dB).

Appendix C: DERIVATION OF NOISE EXPOSURE FRACTION AND TIME-ABOVE EQUATIONS

This Appendix presents a derivation of the noise exposure fraction and time-above equations used in INM 6.0. The assumptions are that the aircraft is on a straight and level flight path flying at constant speed. The equations are based upon a fourth-power, 90-degree dipole model of sound radiation. The geometry for the derivation is shown in Figure C-1.

Figure C-1 Observer/Flight-Path Geometry

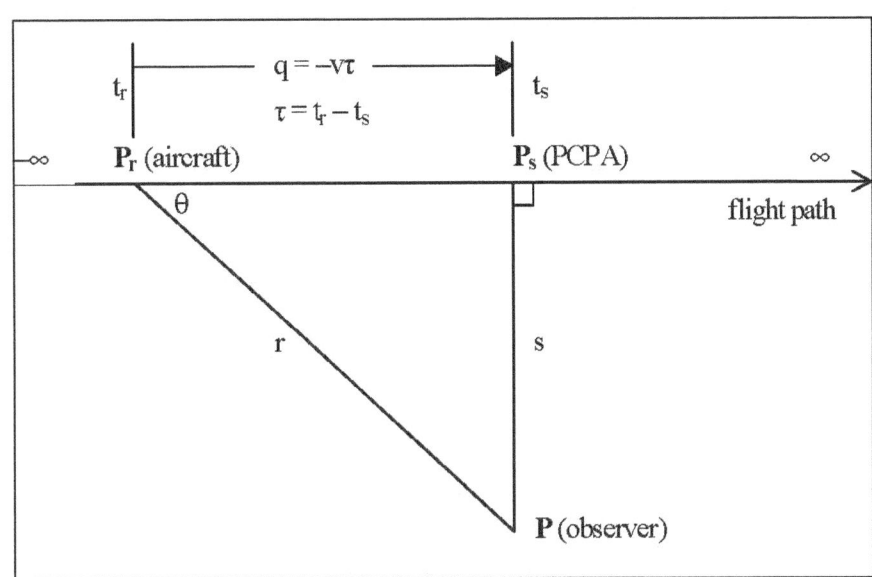

r	distance from the observer at point **P** to the aircraft at point $\mathbf{P_r}$ (feet);
s	perpendicular distance from the observer at point **P** to PCPA at point $\mathbf{P_s}$ (feet);
q	distance along the flight path relative to PCPA (feet);
v	speed of the aircraft (ft/sec);
t_r	time at which the aircraft is located at point $\mathbf{P_r}$ (seconds);
t_s	time at which the aircraft is located at point $\mathbf{P_s}$ (seconds);
τ	time difference, t_r minus t_s (seconds);
θ	angle formed by the flight path and a connecting segment from the aircraft at point $\mathbf{P_r}$ to the observer at point **P**;
p_r	root-mean-square sound pressure generated by the aircraft at point $\mathbf{P_r}$;
p_s	root-mean-square sound pressure generated by the aircraft at point $\mathbf{P_s}$.

The relative distance, q, along the flight path from point $\mathbf{P_r}$ to point $\mathbf{P_s}$ is computed from the scalar product of two vectors: $\mathbf{P_rP}$, from the aircraft to the observer; and the unit vector, $\mathbf{u}$, in the direction of the flight path.

$$q = \mathbf{P_rP} \cdot \mathbf{u} = \mathbf{P_rP} \cdot \mathbf{P_rP_s} / \left| \mathbf{P_rP_s} \right|.$$

The value of q is positive if the aircraft is located behind PCPA (as pictured in the figure), and the value of q is negative if the aircraft is ahead of PCPA. In terms of speed and time, $q = -v\tau$. The negative sign is because τ is negative when the aircraft is behind PCPA.

The noise fraction algorithm is derived from a fourth-power, 90-degree dipole time history model. In this model, p_r^2 is the mean-square sound pressure at the observer due to the aircraft, located at point $\mathbf{P_r}$; and p_s^2 is the mean-square sound pressure at the observer when the aircraft is located at PCPA at point $\mathbf{P_s}$. The mean-square pressure, p_r^2, at the observer is expressed in terms of p_s^2 by

$$p_r^2 = p_s^2 (s^2/r^2) \sin^2\theta$$

which becomes

$$p_r^2 = p_s^2 s^4/r^4.$$

In this equation, the mean-square sound pressure for an aircraft flying along a straight path is determined by r^2 spherical spreading loss and by a $\sin^2\theta$ "90-degree dipole" term that accounts for a variety of physical phenomena. These phenomena include atmospheric absorption, which is accentuated in front of the airplane due to Doppler shift, sound refraction away from the hot gases behind the airplane, and ground attenuation. The purpose of the dipole term is to shape the sides of the time-history curve to fit empirical data.[16] When the $\sin\theta$ term is replaced by s/r, the mean-square sound pressure is seen to vary inversely as r^4; therefore, another name for the model is the "fourth-power" time-history model.

By writing

$$r^2 = s^2 + q^2$$
$$r^2 = s^2 + (v\tau)^2$$
$$(r/s)^2 = 1 + (v\tau/s)^2$$

the mean-square pressure is derived as a function of time

$$p_r^2(\tau) = p_s^2 / (1 + (v\tau/s)^2)^2.$$

The integral of the mean-square pressure, from time τ_1 to τ_2, is the segment noise exposure E_{12}

$$E_{12} = \int_{\tau_1}^{\tau_2} p_r^2(\tau)\, d\tau.$$

By using the substitution

$$\alpha = v\tau/s$$

the segment noise exposure integral becomes

$$E_{12} = p_s^2 (s/v) \int_{\alpha_1}^{\alpha_2} (1 + \alpha^2)^{-2}\, d\alpha$$

and its solution is

$$E_{12} = p_s^2 (s/v)\, \tfrac{1}{2}\{[\alpha_2/(1+\alpha_2^2) + \tan^{-1}\alpha_2] - [\alpha_1/(1+\alpha_1^2) + \tan^{-1}\alpha_1]\}.$$

The total noise exposure from $\tau_1 = -\infty$ to $\tau_2 = \infty$ is

$$E_\infty = \tfrac{1}{2}\pi p_s^2 s/v.$$

The <u>noise exposure fraction</u>, F_{12}, is the noise exposure between time τ_1 and τ_2 divided by the total noise exposure:

$$F_{12} = E_{12} / E_\infty$$
$$F_{12} = (1/\pi) [\alpha_2/(1+\alpha_2{}^2) + \tan^{-1}\alpha_2 - \alpha_1/(1+\alpha_1{}^2) - \tan^{-1}\alpha_1] .$$

The next part of the derivation shows how to calculate α_1 and α_2.

The INM NPD database contains noise exposure level data referenced to 160 knots, $L_{E.160}$, and maximum noise level data, L_{Smx}. These noise level data are related to the parameters in the above equations by

$$L_{E.160} = 10 \log_{10}[(v/v_o) E_\alpha / (p_o{}^2 t_o)]$$
$$L_{Smx} = 10 \log_{10}[p_s{}^2 / p_o{}^2]$$

where

$p_o = 20 \ \mu Pa$

$t_o = 1$ sec for L_{AE} and L_{CE}, or 10 sec for L_{EPN}

$v_o = 270.05$ ft/sec (160 knots).

To ensure that the total exposure obtained from the fourth-power time-history model

$$E_\infty = \tfrac{1}{2} \pi p_s{}^2 s/v$$

is consistent with INM NPD data, the following relationship must hold:

$$L_{E.160} - L_{Smx} = 10 \log_{10}[(v/v_o) (\tfrac{1}{2} \pi p_s{}^2 s/v) / (p_o{}^2 t_o)] - 10 \log_{10}[p_s{}^2 / p_o{}^2].$$

Therefore

$$\tfrac{1}{2} \pi s/(v_o t_o) = 10^{[L_{E.160} - L_{Smx}]/10}$$

and the distance, s, is scaled to fit the NPD data:

$$s = (2/\pi)v_o t_o 10^{[L_{E.160} - L_{Smx}]/10} .$$

Using the symbol s_L to indicated a scaled distance, rather than the actual distance, the NPD-consistency requirement becomes

$$s_L = s_o 10^{[L_{E.160} - L_{Smx}]/10}$$

where the value of the constant depends on the type of noise exposure level:

$s_o = 171.92$ feet for L_{AE} and L_{CE}

$s_o = 1719.2$ feet for L_{EPN}.

Using the scaled distance, s_L, and the definition $\alpha = v\tau/s = -q/s$, the two α-numbers that are needed to calculate the noise exposure fraction, F_{12}, are determined by $q = q_1$ at the start of a segment:

$$\alpha_1 = -q_1/s_L$$
$$\alpha_2 = (-q_1 + L)/s_L$$

where

q_1 relative distance (feet) from segment start point to point $\mathbf{P_s}$

L length of segment (feet).

The next part of the derivation shows how to calculate time-above.

Using the previously developed time-history equation and substituting $s = s_L$, the mean-square pressure is written as a function of time, τ, and speed, v:

$$p_r^2 = p_s^2 / (1 + (v\tau/s_L)^2)^2 .$$

The time-history equation is solved for τ as a function of p_r:

$$\tau = (s_L/v)(p_s/p_r - 1)^{\frac{1}{2}} .$$

Given a noise threshold level, L_x, of root-mean-square pressure, p_x,

$$L_x = 10 \log_{10}[p_x^2/p_o^2]$$

the time duration during which the noise level exceeds L_x, Δt_x, is twice the τ-value at $p_r = p_x$:

$$\Delta t_x = 2(s_L/v)[(p_s^2/p_x^2)^{\frac{1}{2}} - 1]^{\frac{1}{2}} \qquad \text{(seconds)},$$

which can be written as

$$\Delta t_x = 2(s_L/v)[10^{[L_{Smx.adj} - L_x]/20} - 1]^{\frac{1}{2}} \qquad (L_x < L_{Smx.adj})$$

where $L_{Smx.adj}$ is the adjusted maximum noise level at the observer. If the maximum noise level is less than the threshold, the time duration is zero.

Note that

$$s_L/v = (2/\pi)(t_o v_o/v) 10^{[L_{E.160.adj} - L_{Smx.adj}]/10}$$

and that

$$L_{E.adj} = L_{E.160.adj} + 10 \log_{10}[v_o/v]$$

where

$L_{E.160.adj}$	adjusted noise exposure level referenced to 160 knots,
$L_{E.adj}$	adjusted noise exposure level at the observer,
$L_{Smx.adj}$	adjusted maximum noise level at the observer.

Then, the <u>time-above duration</u> equation can be written in terms of adjusted exposure and maximum levels:

$$\Delta t_x = (4/\pi) t_o 10^{[L_{E.adj} - L_{Smx.adj}]/10}[10^{[L_{Smx.adj} - L_x]/20} - 1]^{\frac{1}{2}} / 60 \qquad \text{(minutes)}.$$

Appendix D: OVERVIEW OF SPECTRAL CLASS DEVELOPMENT

This appendix provides an example of the derivation of a spectral class for the INM database. Departure spectral class #104 is used in this example. The class originally consisted of the Fokker F28-2000, the McDonnell-Douglas MD80 series aircraft (i.e., MD81, MD82 and MD83), and the Gulfstream GIIB and GIII twin-engine, high bypass ratio turbofan aircraft. The original development and assignment of spectral classes was performed in 1999 and documented in Reference 13.

The hushkit retrofitted B737N17 and B737N19 have NPD curves referenced to spectral class 104. They were added to the INM database after the original derivations were performed and were found to agree with an already developed class based on the criteria described in Step 1 through Step 4 below.

Step 1: Group Similar Aircraft/Engine Combinations

The first step in deriving a spectral class is the grouping of aircraft considered similar based on the combination of the aircraft and engine types. Considerations for grouping aircraft include the airframe, type of engine, number of engines, location of engine, and bypass ratio.

Step 2: Visual Inspection of Potential Spectral Class Data

After having grouped the aircraft by similar aircraft/engine types, the maximum-level spectra are compared. Specifically, each spectrum at the time of A-weighted Maximum Sound Level (L_{ASmx}) is graphed on a single chart and visually inspected for similarity. Similarity is based on the shape of the spectrum and the relative location of any tones below 1000 Hz. The spectra for class 104 are presented in Figure D-1

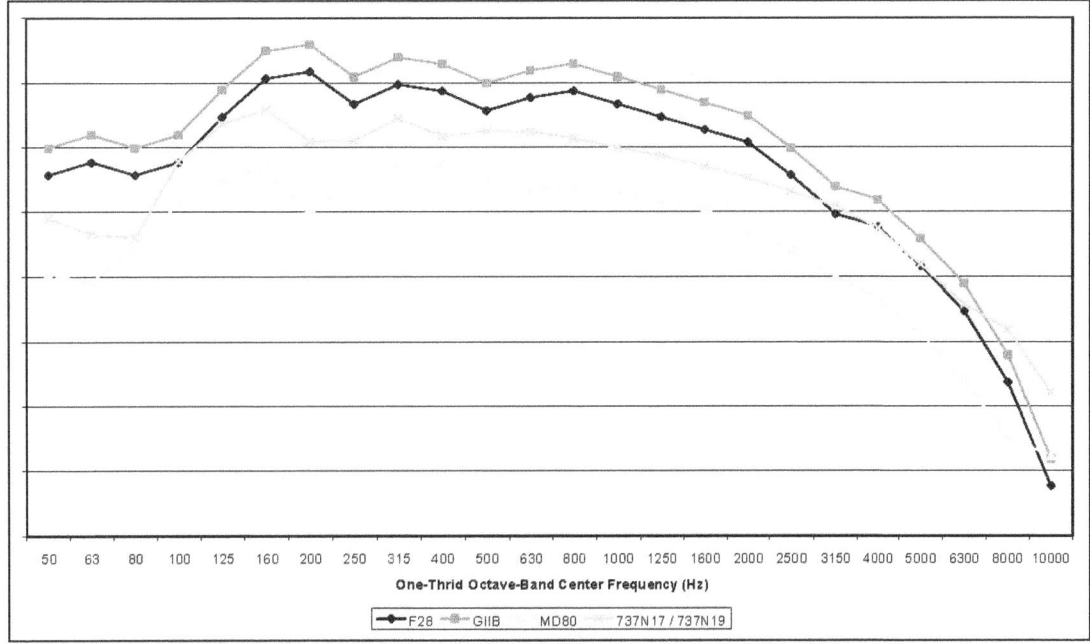

Figure D-1 Departure Class 104

To aid in the visual inspection of the spectra, each one is normalized to a value of 70 dB at 1000 Hz. Figure D-2 presents the normalized spectra along with the *proposed* spectrum that would represent this spectral class. The representative spectrum for this spectral class is the weighted arithmetic average of the individual one-third octave-band spectral data. The weighting was based on a recent annual survey of the number of departures for each aircraft type.

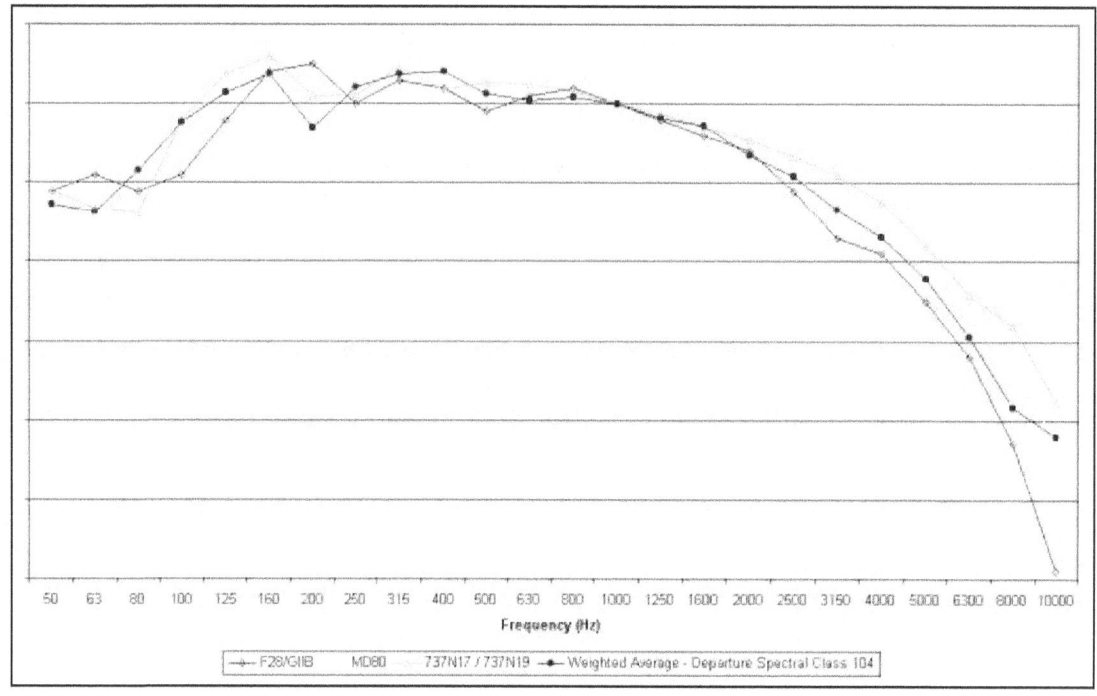

Figure D-2 Normalized Spectral Class 104 Data

Step 3: Verification of Proposed Spectral Class

In order to verify the appropriateness of the proposed spectral class, the individual spectra and the representative spectrum are used in a series of acoustical calculations that require third-octave band spectra data. One example is the algorithm that calculates the theoretical ground effect for a source-to-receiver separation distance of 1000m. The EPD Model (see References 24 through 26), which was originally documented by Tony Embleton, Joe Piercy and Giles Daigle of the National Research Council in Canada, was used. This model employs spectral data to calculate the ground effect for propagation over ground with different effective flow resistivities. A flow resistivity of 150 cgs rayls (essentially soft ground cover) was used for this validation.

Figure D-3 presents the calculated ground effects as a function of source-to- receiver elevation angle for the proposed representative spectrum and the individual aircraft spectra. Additionally, limit curves are drawn ±1 dB from the proposed representative spectrum ground effect. The proposed representative spectrum is considered appropriate to represent the spectral class if the ground effect curves for each aircraft generally fall within the proposed representative spectrum limit curves for all elevation angles.

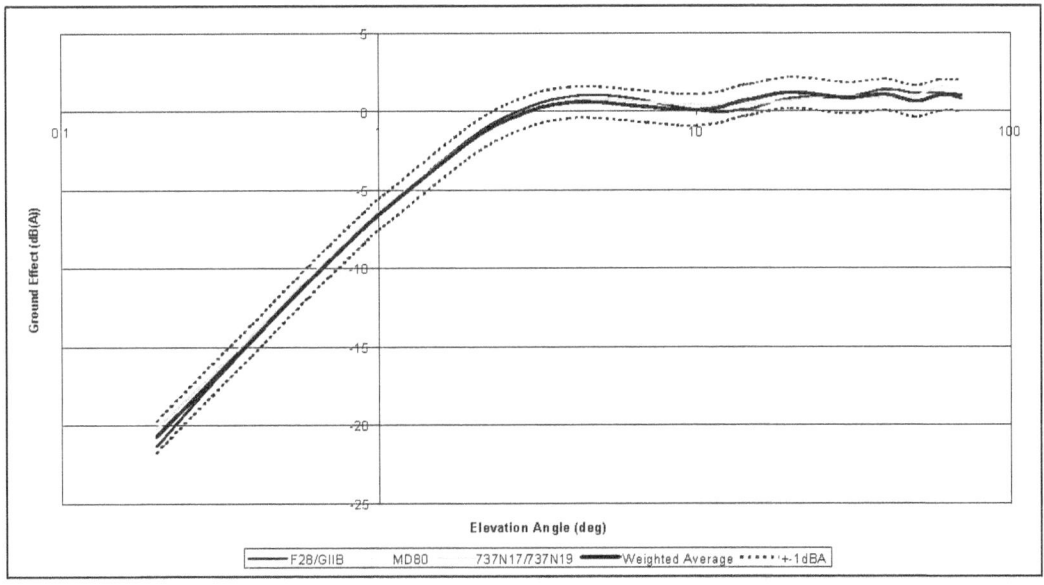

Figure D-3 Spectral Class 104 Ground Effect

Step 4: Final Spectral Class

Given that the ground effect curves for each individual aircraft spectrum fall within the ±1-dB limit curves for all elevation angles, the proposed representative spectrum is considered to adequately represent the individual spectra used to derive the spectral class. Figure D-4 presents the final spectral class.

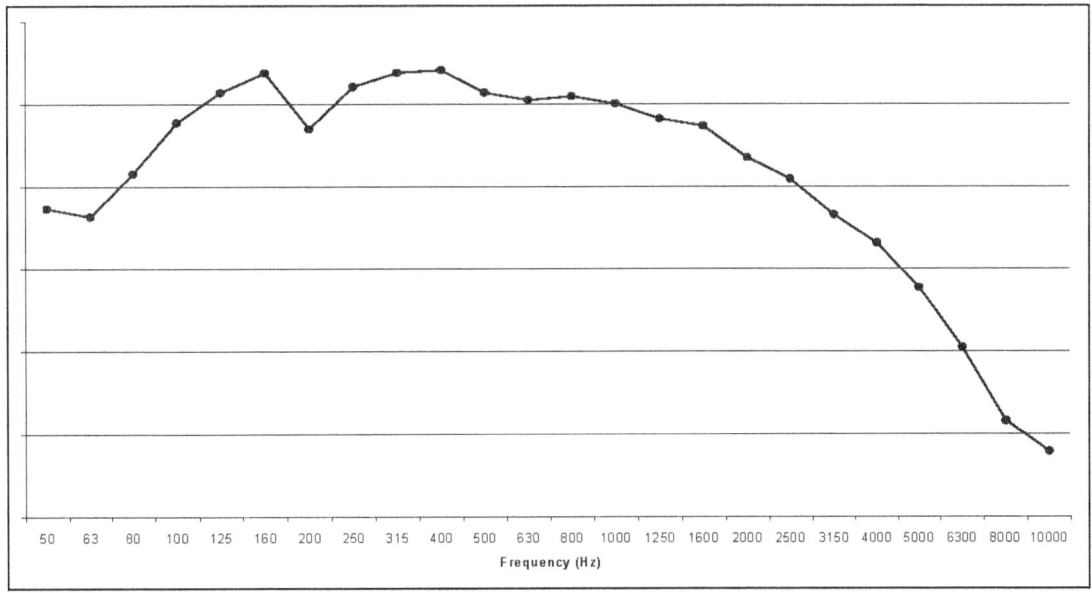

Figure D-4 Departure Spectral Class 104

Appendix E: INM Database Request Form

The following describes the performance and noise data required for aircraft to be included in the FAA's INM database.

1. REFERENCE CONDITIONS FOR PERFORMANCE DATA

Wind	4 m/s (8 kt) headwind, constant with height above ground
Runway elevation	Mean Sea Level (MSL)
Runway gradient	None
Air temperature	15°C (59°F)
Aircraft takeoff gross weight	85% of maximum takeoff weight
Aircraft landing weight	90% of maximum landing weight
Number of engines supplying thrust	All
Atmosphere	International Standard Atmosphere (ISA)

2. AIRCRAFT AND ENGINE DATA

Where there are variations in certification weights and engine thrusts for a given model, provide data for the heaviest aircraft in terms of maximum gross takeoff weight in the model classification.

Aircraft model	
Engine model	
Number of engines	
Engine type (jet, turboprop, piston)	
Noise stage number (2, 3, 4)	
Maximum static thrust (lb/engine)	
Automated thrust restoration (yes, no)	
Weight class (small, large, heavy)	
Maximum gross takeoff weight (lb)	
Maximum gross landing weight (lb)	
Maximum landing distance (ft)	

Departure Takeoff Weights

Stage number	Trip length (nmi)	Weight (lb)
1	0-500	lb
2	500-1000	lb
3	1000-1500	lb
4	1500-2500	lb
5	2500-3500	lb
6	3500-4500	lb
7	>4500	lb

Takeoff weights should be developed so as to increase with an increase in mission trip length. Weight assumptions should use industry planning assumptions for load factor, average passenger weight, excess cargo beyond passenger weight, and fuel required to complete mission trip length.

3. AERODYNAMIC COEFFICIENTS

Aerodynamic coefficients for use with the SAE AIR 1845 equations are required for available flap settings. The flap settings may be identified in degrees and abbreviations. Please provide data for all flap settings specified in Sections 5 and 6.

Flap Configuration Identifier	Operation (A, D)[1]	Gear	Takeoff **B** (ft/lb)	Takeoff **C** (kt/√lb)	Land **D** (kt/√lb)	Drag/Lift **R**
	D	down				
	D	down				
	D	up	[2]			
	D	up				
	D	up				
	A	up				
	A	up				
	A	down				
	A	down				
	A	down				

[1] A = Approach, D = Depart
[2] Not applicable

4. ENGINE COEFFICIENTS

For jet aircraft, engine coefficients in accordance with SAE AIR 1845 equations are required for maximum takeoff, maximum climb, and general thrust in terms of EPR or N1. The Max-Takeoff coefficients should be valid to 6,000 ft MSL, the Max-Climb and General Thrust coefficients should be valid to 16,000 ft MSL. This is necessary so that the INM accurately models operations at high altitude airports such as Denver and Salt Lake City.

In addition, high temperature coefficients are required for operations above the thrust break temperature. INM uses the Max-Takeoff and Max-Climb coefficients below the breakpoint temperature and uses the Hi-Temp coefficients above the breakpoint temperature. The breakpoint temperature is at the intersection of the two curves. An example of Max-Takeoff and Hi-Temp Max-Takeoff curves is shown in Figure E-1.

Thrust Type	E (lb)	F (lb/kt)	Ga (lb/ft)	Gb (lb/ft^2)	H (lb/°C)
Max-Takeoff					
Hi-Temp Max-Takeoff					
Max-Climb					
Hi-Temp Max-Climb					
General Thrust					
Hi-Temp General Thrust					
	K1a (lb/EPR)	K1b (lb/EPR^2)	or	K2 lb/(N1/√θ)	K3 lb/(N1/√θ)^2
General Thrust					
Hi-Temp General Thrust					

For propeller-driven aircraft, engine coefficients in accordance with SAE AIR 1845 equations are required for propeller efficiency and installed net propulsive power.

Thrust Type	Propeller Efficiency	Installed net propulsive horsepower (hp)
Max-Takeoff		
Max-Climb		

5. DEPARTURE PROCEDURES

Departure procedures consist of a takeoff segment, and a combination of climb and acceleration segments up to an altitude of 10,000 ft AFE. A climb segment is defined by its endpoint altitude. An acceleration segment is defined by its rate-of-climb and the calibrated airspeed at its endpoint. The flap settings are indicated for endpoints of segments. These flap settings should coincide with those given in Section 3 above. Please provide procedural data for each stage length given in Section 2 above.

Stage Number	

Repeat table for each takeoff stage number (takeoff weight) listed in Section 2

Segment Type[1]	Thrust Type[2] (T/C)	Flap Configuration Identifier[3]	Endpoint Altitude (ft AFE)	Rate-of-Climb (ft/min)	Endpoint Speed (KCAS)	Start Thrust[4] (lb)
Takeoff						lb
Climb			ft			lb
Accelerate				fpm	kt	lb
Accelerate				fpm	kt	lb
Climb						lb
Accelerate				fpm	kt	lb
Climb			ft			lb
Climb			ft			lb
Climb			10000			lb

[1] Add, delete, and sequence the segments as necessary to represent a takeoff procedure.
[2] T = Max-Takeoff, C = Max-Climb, as defined in Section 4.
[3] Use the identifiers in Section 3.
[4] These data are used to compare to INM-computed thrust values.

6. APPROACH PROCEDURES

A landing profile should be calculated for a starting altitude of 6000 feet above field elevation
(AFE). The flap settings should coincide with those given in Section 3 above.

Landing weight (lb)	lb
Stopping distance (ft)	ft

Profile Point	Operation	Altitude (ft AFE)	Distance from Touchdown[1] (ft)	Start Speed (KTAS)	Flap Configuration[2]	Start Thrust[3] (lb)
1	Descend	6000	-114487	kt		lb
2	Descend	3000	-57243	kt		lb
3	Descend	1500	-28622	kt		lb
4	Descend	1000	-19081	kt		lb
5	Land	0	0	[4]kt		lb
6	Reverse Thrust	0	ft	kt		lb
7	Start Taxi	0	ft	kt		lb

[1] Glide slope is 3.0 degrees.

[2] Use identifiers in Section 3.

[3] These data are used to compare to INM-computed thrust values.

[4] Landing speed is for reference only; INM calculates landing speed using the D coefficient (Section 3) and
landing weight.

7. NOISE DATA

Noise Power Distance (NPD) data are requested for noise exposure levels (Sound Exposure Level and Effective Perceived Noise Level) and maximum noise levels (Maximum A-weighted Sound Level and Maximum Tone-Corrected Perceived Noise Level). NPD data should be provided for representative corrected net thrust values for both approach and departure operations over a set of 10 distances. Noise levels should be adjusted for spherical spreading, distance duration, time-varying aircraft speed, and atmospheric absorption in accordance with the methodology presented in SAE AIR 1845.

Noise Type[1]	
Operation[2]	

Repeat table for each combination of noise type and operation (8 tables)

Distance (ft)	Corrected Net Thrust per Engine (lb)					
	lb	lb	lb	lb	lb	lb
200	dB	dB	dB	dB	dB	dB
400	dB	dB	dB	dB	dB	dB
630	dB	dB	dB	dB	dB	dB
1000	dB	dB	dB	dB	dB	dB
2000	dB	dB	dB	dB	dB	dB
4000	dB	dB	dB	dB	dB	dB
6300	dB	dB	dB	dB	dB	dB
10000	dB	dB	dB	dB	dB	dB
16000	dB	dB	dB	dB	dB	dB
25000	dB	dB	dB	dB	dB	dB

[1] NOISE TYPES
L_{AE} = Sound Exposure Level (reference speed 160 kt)
L_{EPN} = Effective Perceived Noise Level (reference speed 160 kt)
L_{ASmx} = Maximum A-weighted Sound Level (at speed close to 160 kt)
L_{PNTSmx} = Maximum Tone-Corrected Perceived Noise Level (at speed close to 160 kt)

[2] OPERATIONS
A = Approach
D = Depart

In addition, tables of third-octave band spectral data are requested, two tables at the time of Maximum A-weighted Sound Level for approach and departure operations, and two tables at the time of Maximum Tone-Corrected Perceived Noise Level for both approach and departure operations. The spectra should be at the same corrected net thrust values as provided in the noise exposure and maximum noise tables. The spectra should be measured at a speed close to 160 knots and adjusted to a reference distance of 1000 feet using the atmospheric absorption table in SAE AIR 1845.

Third-octave band spectra at time[1]	
Operation[2]	

Repeat table for each combination of time and operation (4 tables)

Band (Hz)	Corrected Net Thrust per Engine (lb)					
	lb	lb	lb	lb	lb	lb
50	dB	dB	dB	dB	dB	dB
63	dB	dB	dB	dB	dB	dB
80	dB	dB	dB	dB	dB	dB
100	dB	dB	dB	dB	dB	dB
125	dB	dB	dB	dB	dB	dB
160	dB	dB	dB	dB	dB	dB
200	dB	dB	dB	dB	dB	dB
250	dB	dB	dB	dB	dB	dB
315	dB	dB	dB	dB	dB	dB
400	dB	dB	dB	dB	dB	dB
500	dB	dB	dB	dB	dB	dB
630	dB	dB	dB	dB	dB	dB
800	dB	dB	dB	dB	dB	dB
1000	dB	dB	dB	dB	dB	dB
1250	dB	dB	dB	dB	dB	dB
1600	dB	dB	dB	dB	dB	dB
2000	dB	dB	dB	dB	dB	dB
2500	dB	dB	dB	dB	dB	dB
3150	dB	dB	dB	dB	dB	dB
4000	dB	dB	dB	dB	dB	dB
5000	dB	dB	dB	dB	dB	dB
6300	dB	dB	dB	dB	dB	dB
8000	dB	dB	dB	dB	dB	dB
10000	dB	dB	dB	dB	dB	dB

[1] At time of L_{ASmx} and L_{PNTSmx}
[2] Operation A = Approach and D = Depart

Figure E-1: Example Maximum Takeoff Thrust vs. Temperature

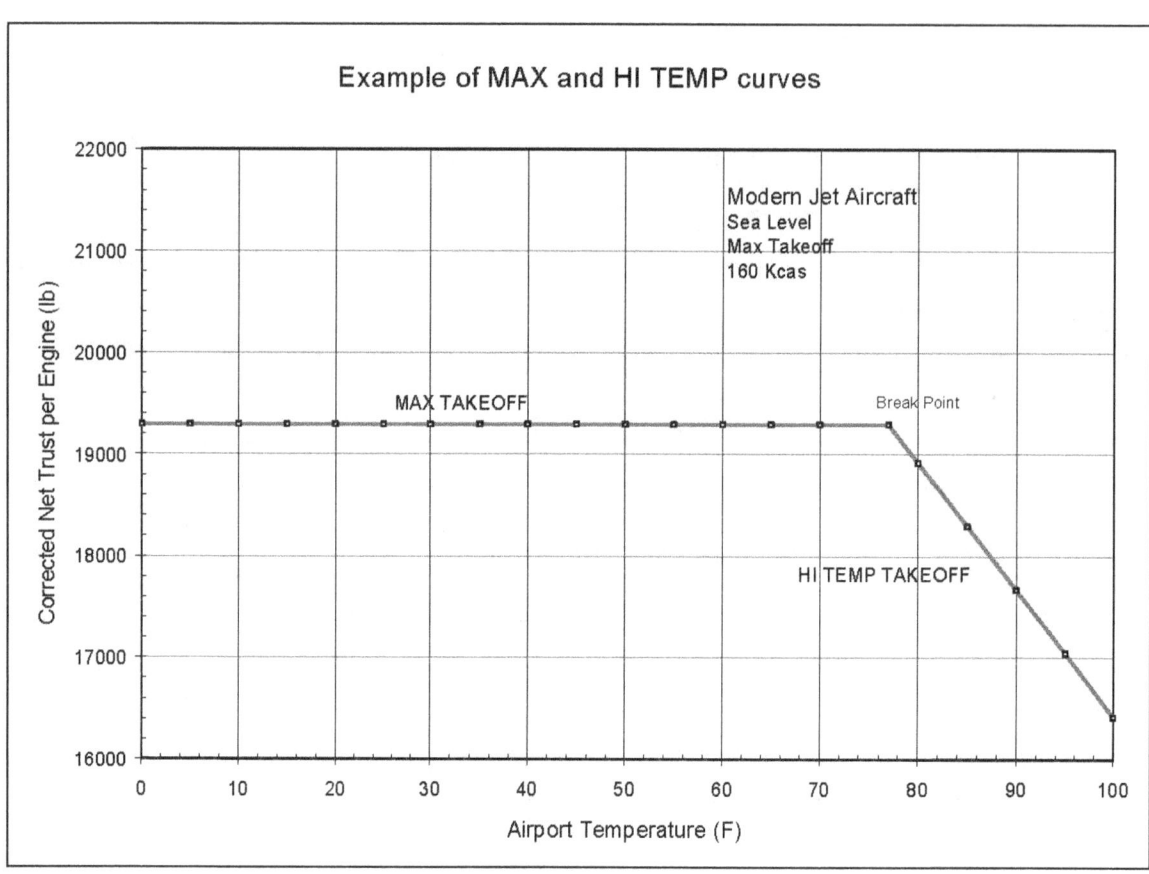

REFERENCES

1. Olmstead, et al., <u>Integrated Noise Model (INM) Version 6.0 User's Guide</u>, Report No. FAA-AEE-99-03, Washington, D.C.: Federal Aviation Administration, September 1999.

2. Newman, J. S., Beattie, K. R., <u>Aviation Noise Effects</u>, Report No. FAA-EE-85-2, Washington, DC: FAA, Office of Environment and Energy, March 1985.

3. Harris, C. M. (ed.), <u>Handbook of Acoustical Measurements and Noise Control</u>, Third Edition, New York, NY: McGraw-Hill, 1991.

4. Beranek, L. L., (ed.), <u>Noise and Vibration Control</u>, Revised Edition, New York, NY: McGraw-Hill, 1988.

5. <u>Acoustical Terminology, American National Standard</u>, ANSI S1.1-1994, New York, NY: American National Standards Institute, 1994.

6. Bennett, R. L., Pearsons, K. S., <u>Handbook of Aircraft Noise Metrics</u>, NASA Contractor Report No. 3406, Canoga Park, CA: Bolt Beranek and Newman Inc., 1981.

7. Society of Automotive Engineers, Committee A-21, Aircraft Noise, <u>Standard Values of Atmospheric Absorption as a Function of Temperature and Humidity</u>, Aerospace Research Report No. 866A, Warrendale, PA: Society of Automotive Engineers, Inc., March 1975.

8. Society of Automotive Engineers, Committee A-21, Aircraft Noise, <u>Procedure for the Computation of Airplane Noise in the Vicinity of Airports</u>, Aerospace Information Report No. 1845, Warrendale, PA: Society of Automotive Engineers, Inc., March 1986.

9. International Civil Aviation Organization, <u>Manual of the ICAO Standard Atmosphere</u>, Doc 7488/3, 1993.

10. <u>Federal Aviation Regulations, Part 36, Noise Standards: Aircraft Type and Airworthiness Certification</u>, Washington, D.C.: Federal Aviation Administration, September 1992.

11. Moulton, C .L., <u>Air Force Procedure for Predicting Aircraft Noise Around Airbases: Noise Exposure Model (NOISEMAP)</u>, User's Manual, Report No. AAMRL-TR-90-011, Wright-Patterson Air Force Base, Ohio: United States Air Force, February 1990.

12. Bishop, D. E., Beckmann, J. M., Bucka, M. P., <u>Revision of Civil Aircraft Noise Data for the Integrated Noise Model (INM)</u>, Report No. 6039, Canoga Park, CA: BBN Laboratories Incorporated, September 1986.

13. Spectral Classes For FAA's Integrated Noise Model, Report No. DTS-34-FA065-LR1, Cambridge, MA, John A. Volpe National Transportation Systems Center, December 1999.

14. Connor, et. al., Accuracy of the Integrated Noise Model (INM): MD-80 Operational Noise Levels, Washington, D.C.: Federal Aviation Administration and Swedish Civil Aviation Administration, May 1995.

15. Wei-Nian Su, John-Paul Clarke, Aircraft Performance Algorithms in INM, Cambridge, MA: Department of Aeronautics and Astronautics, Massachusetts Institute of Technology.

16. Eldred, K. M., Miller, R. L., Analysis of Selected Topics in the Methodology of the Integrated Noise Model, Report No. 4413, BBN Project No. 09611, Cambridge, MA: Bolt Beranek and Newman Inc., September 1980.

17. Boeing Commercial Airplane Company, Boeing Airplane/Noise Performance Computer Program - Programmer's Manual, Report No. FAA-EQ-73-7.7, Seattle, WA: Boeing Commercial Airplane Company, December 1973.

18. Kurzweil, L., Relationship Between Atmospheric Temperature, Pressure, Density, Speed of Sound and Altitude When Airport Temperature and Elevation are Prescribed, Memorandum to Thomas L. Connor, FAA/AEE-120, Cambridge, MA: Transportation Systems Center, February 1986.

19. Kurzweil, L., Computation of Fraction (F_{12}) of Data-Base Noise Level Represented by a Finite Length Flight Segment, INM Technical Overview and Work Plan, Cambridge, MA: Transportation Systems Center, March 1987.

20. Eldred, K. M., Approximating Aircraft Noise Using a Model of a Moving Source with a 90° Dipole Radiation Pattern, Memorandum to Dr. R. G. Gados, The Mitre Corporation, Cambridge, MA: Bolt Beranek and Newman, Inc., March 1980.

21. Society of Automotive Engineers, Committee A-21, Aircraft Noise, Prediction Method for Lateral Attenuation of Airplane Noise During Takeoff and Landing, Aerospace Information Report No. 1751, Warrendale, PA: Society of Automotive Engineers, Inc., March 1981.

22. Wasmer, F., NMPLOT Version 4.6 Computer Program, Champaign, IL: Wasmer Consulting, October, 2000.

23. Anderson, G. S., Lee, C. S. Y., Fleming, G. G., Menge, C. W., FHWA Traffic Noise Model (FHWA TNM®), User's Guide, Version 1.0, Report No. FHWA-PD-96-009, Cambridge, MA: John A. Volpe National Transportation Systems Center, August 1996.

24. Embleton, Tony F.W., Piercy, Joe E., Daigle, Giles A., Effective Flow Resistivity of Ground Surfaces Determined by Acoustical Measurements, Journal of the Acoustical Society of America 74(4), 1239-1243 (1983).

25. Embleton, Tony F.W., <u>Sound Propagation Outdoors- Improved Prediction Schemes for the 80's</u>, Noise Control Engineering Journal, 18(1), 30-39 (1982).

26. Embleton, Tony F.W., Piercy, Joe E., Daigle, Giles A., <u>Outdoor Propagation Over Ground of Finite Impedance</u>, Journal of the Acoustical Society of America 59(2), 267-277 (1976).

www.ingramcontent.com/pod-product-compliance
Lightning Source LLC
Chambersburg PA
CBHW081110290526
45795CB00006B/2070